Floppy Toys

FLOPPY TOYS

by Brenda Morton

with drawings by Juliet Renny
and photographs by Stephen Moreton-Prichard

FABER AND FABER
3 QUEEN SQUARE, LONDON

First published in 1970
by Faber and Faber Limited
3 Queen Square London WC1
Reprinted 1971
Printed in Great Britain by
Latimer Trend & Co Ltd Whitstable

ISBN 0 571 09495 3

Contents

Illustrations

HORIZONTAL

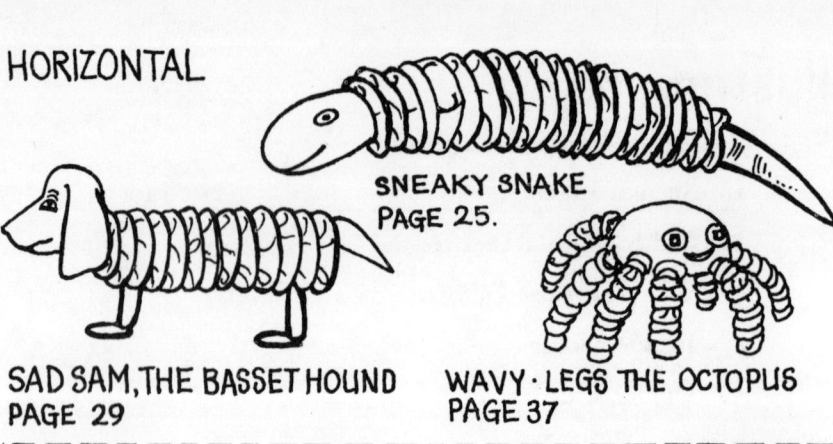

SNEAKY SNAKE
PAGE 25.

SAD SAM, THE BASSET HOUND
PAGE 29

WAVY · LEGS THE OCTOPUS
PAGE 37

UPRIGHT

DINKIE MOUSE
PAGE 41

UGGLIE,
A CAVEMAN
PAGE 46

WITH ARMS

WEE WILLIE WINKIE
PAGE 50

SANTA CLAUS
PAGE 59

TOPSYTURVY
BRIDESMAID (turn her over) GYPSY
PAGE 70

WITH ARMS AND LEGS

TUMBLER
THE CLOWN
PAGE 82

FOOTBALLER
or ordinary boy
PAGE 91

LITTLE RED
RIDING HOOD
or ordinary girl
PAGE 97

MICKEY MONKEY
PAGE 106

FOUR LEGGED ANIMALS

FRISKY LAMB. PAGE 114

SINGH THE TIGER. PAGE 119

KNITTED

JOSEPH IN HIS COAT
OF MANY COLOURS
PAGE 125

9

Introduction
What are Floppy Toys?

Floppy toys are made from circles of material, gathered and threaded on elastic.

This method gives the toys an unusual appearance: appealing, charming and funny. Pull the limbs or head to stretch the elastic and then watch it ping back! It fascinates adults, and children will play at it for hours. The head and limbs can revolve. Sometimes the hands, feet and tail as well. Nobody really wants a monkey with its head looking backwards but it adds to the fun to be able to turn it round. The toys are extra cuddly and the sausage shape of the gathered circles has an unusual feel which is very cuddly and appealing.

The cost is negligible. The circles use such small scraps of material that the toys can be made from dressmaking cuttings or tiny oddments. Most of the toys can be made from circles of assorted colours (see page 135): a pile of scraps in a multitude of colours can make a very attractive toy. They are washable: ordinary dressmaking materials are used with plastic foam for stuffing head and extremities. The toys can also be knitted, using up small balls of different coloured wools (see page 132).

Little stuffing is needed. Some toymakers dislike doing stuffing and in these toys only the heads and extremities are stuffed. *Ugglie, a Caveman* does not have any at all.

Sew the circles at leisure. No concentration is needed for gathering the circles. So take a pile of them with you when sitting in the garden, on a picnic, or on holiday. People whose hands are weak or stiff can gather the circles, which are small and light to handle. Stronger hands are needed to thread and sew the elastic, but help in preparing the circles is always welcome. These toys are not for workers who must have rapid results. Gathering a large pile of circles can take time. The ideal method is to do them at odd moments as already suggested, then the rest of the work and assembly take a normal amount of time.

Quickest toys:	Dinkie Mouse: Santa Claus: Ugglie, a Caveman.
Most adaptable:	Sneaky Snake is adaptable not only in colours by in size. Make the head and tail, then sew circles until time runs out. A short snake still looks like a snake.
Slowest:	Mickey Monkey: Wavy Legs the Octopus.

They are suitable for making in schools though the biggest toys are better avoided, unless circles are taken home to sew. Pupils who finish a basic garment more quickly than their classmates could make a floppy toy from the cuttings. Plastic foam chips for stuffing are not very suitable for school classrooms as they are liable to fly about and cling to tables and clothes. The individual at home can cope with this, but schools would be better advised to use kapok.

Four-legged animals can be made to sit, or to cuddle, but they will not stand unaided. Toys intended as mascots for teenagers or adults can be threaded with wire when they should stand, but without elastic they will not ping. Wire is not suitable for babies.

When somebody is playing with a toy and pinging it a gap may frequently appear between the circles. The reason is usually that the circles have been squeezed closer together. Do not panic! Just pull the circles back along the gap and all is well. A child can enjoy doing this nearly as much as pinging the toy.

The elastic will perish in time but emergency doors are provided which make the elastic accessible for rethreading.

The toys are very individual; no two need ever be alike. The threaded circles give scope for combining different shades of one colour and different patterns in one body, or combining contrasting colours to give striped effects (see 'Imagination with Material', page 135). Different thicknesses of fabric will produce a bigger or smaller toy, without changing the size or number of the circles. Footballer made in cottons that varied just a little in stiffness produced two distinct sizes of toy: big brother and little brother.

General Instructions

CIRCLES FOR YOU TO TRACE

Place folded edge of tracing paper on the diameter line. Trace semi-circle of required diameter, cut out and unfold circle pattern (Fig. 1).

FABRIC

Any suitable fabric can be used.
Different fabrics can be used in the same toy.

FABRIC TO AVOID

Thick cloth. It will not gather well.
Anything that frays easily. If in doubt, try gathering one circle to test it. Then make a hole for the elastic and pull circle from different directions to see if material stays firm.

PATTERNS

All diagrams are traced straight from the book.
Instructions give the size and number of small pieces required so that oddments from dressmaking cuttings and the rag bag can be fitted to the pattern.
The total quantity of material is given at the end of each list for anyone wishing to buy fabric to obtain a special effect.

STUFFING

The plastic foam chips are sold in large plastic bags, which contain enough for a number of toys. Where to buy them will depend on local conditions but try drapers and handicraft suppliers. At the time of writing they can also be bought by mail order from Limericks, the household linen suppliers, of Hamlet Court Road, Westcliff-on-Sea, Essex.

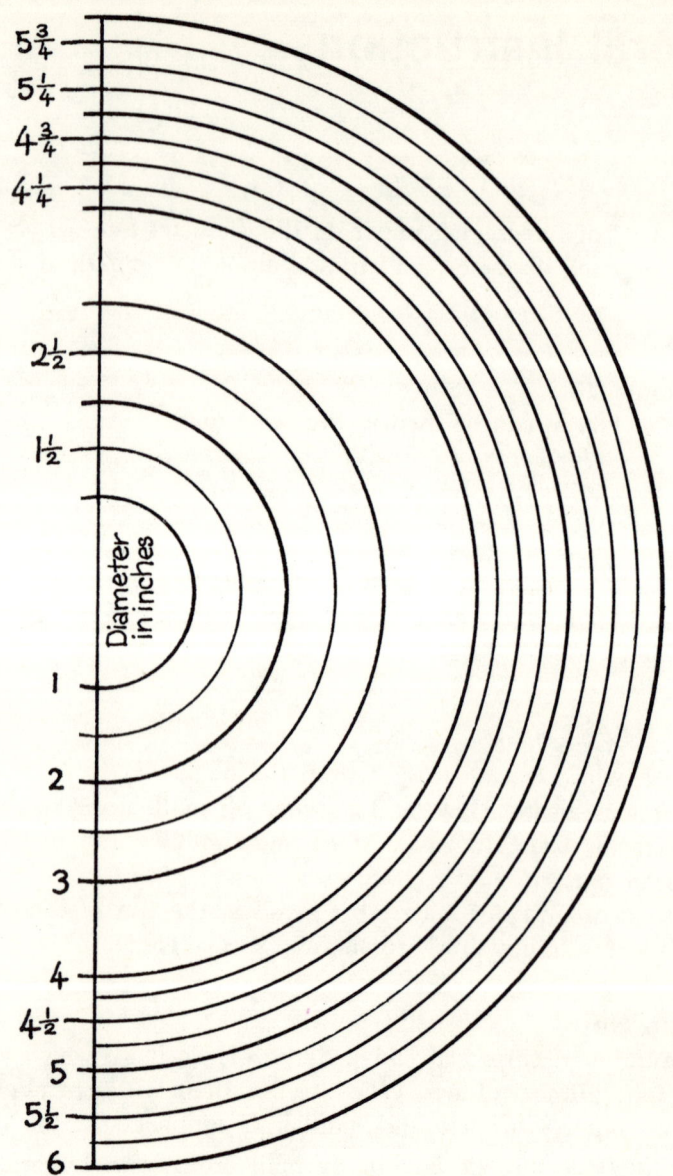

Diameter in inches

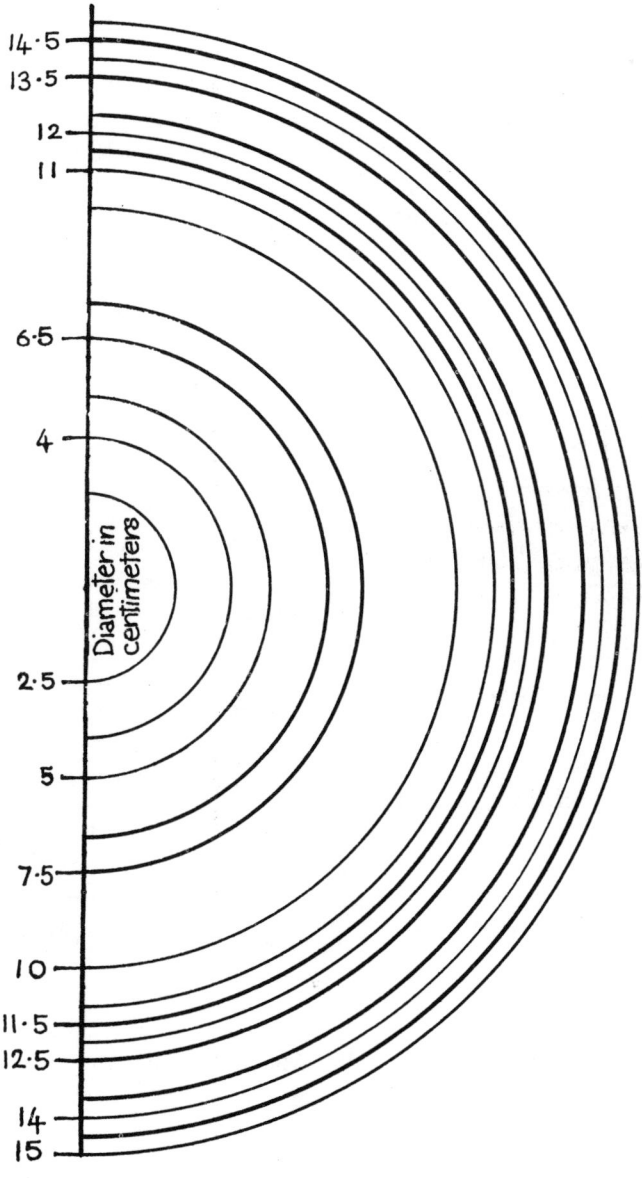

Diameter in centimeters

14·5
13·5
12
11
6·5
4
2·5
5
7·5
10
11·5
12·5
14
15

15

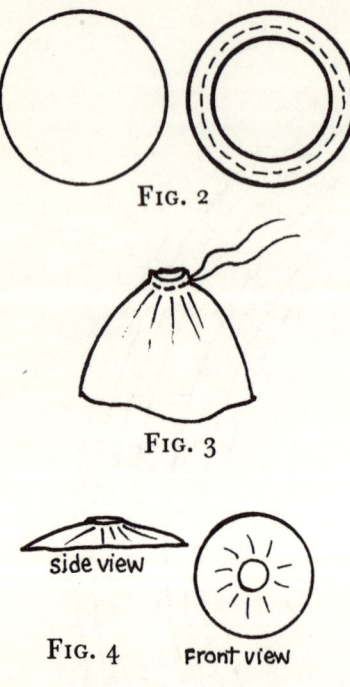

FIG. 2

FIG. 3

side view

FIG. 4   Front view

Cut circle of material. Turn edge over to wrong side, about $\frac{1}{8}$ in (*3 mm*). Gather close to fold. Use thread double.

Pull up as tight as possible, so that raw edges go to inside. Right side is now outside. Finish off thread on gathered seam.
Do not take stitches backwards and forwards across central hole, which must be left free for elastic.

Flatten material to form flat circle. Just press it with fingers. Do not iron it: ironing flattens it and reduces the bulk; much of the cuddly feel is lost and at least one-third more circles are needed to give comparable length of toy.

THREADING THE ELASTIC

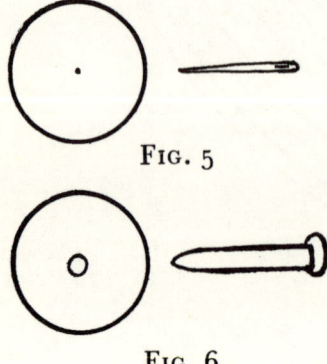

FIG. 5

FIG. 6

Work on smooth side of gathered circle. Prick hole in centre with thick needle. Yarn or wool needle is best. If not available use thick darning needle.

Enlarge hole with point of thick knitting needle.
Work from smooth side so that edges of hole are pushed towards the gathers.

FIG. 7

Thread elastic through hole using wide-eyed yarn or darning needle. By this method elastic threads easily.

Flat knicker elastic is the most satisfactory type to use. Use black or white, whichever will blend better with the material.

Measures given with patterns are approximate. As materials vary in thickness different lengths may be needed so it is advisable to calculate length of elastic required, as follows.

CALCULATING LENGTH OF ELASTIC

A. *Thread circles on tacking thread*
B. *Straight sections*

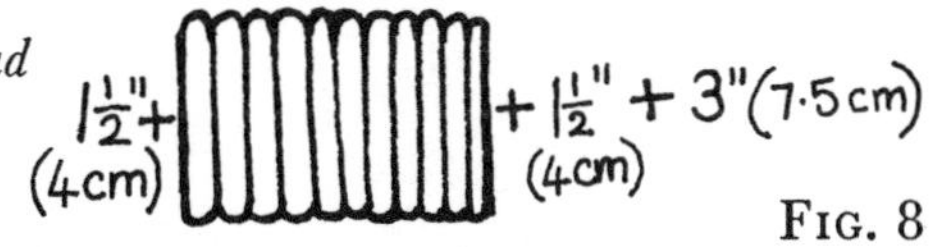

$1\frac{1}{2}$" + (4 cm) [coil] + $1\frac{1}{2}$" + 3"(7·5 cm) (4 cm)

FIG. 8

Measure length. Add 6 in (*or 15·5 cm*):
$1\frac{1}{2}$ in (*4 cm*) for starting tail.
$1\frac{1}{2}$ in (*4 cm*) for finishing tail.
3 in (*7·5 cm*) for ease of handling at end.

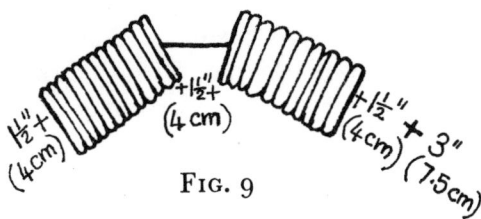

FIG. 9

Arms, or legs for four-legged animals
Two arms or legs are made in one unit.
Thread one arm or leg.
Double measure. Add $7\frac{1}{2}$ in (*or 19·5 cm*):
$2 \times 1\frac{1}{2}$ in (*4 cm*) for starting tail at each wrist or ankle.
$1\frac{1}{2}$ in (*4 cm*) for central part to sew to body.
3 in (*7·5 cm*) for ease of handling at end.

17

Body and legs

One length of elastic folded in half. Thread body and one leg.

Double measure. Add 10½ in (*or 27 cm*):

1½ in (*4 cm*) for starting loop at neck.

2 × 1½ in (*4 cm*) for finishing tail at each ankle.

2 × 3 in (*7.5 cm*) for ease of handling at each ankle.

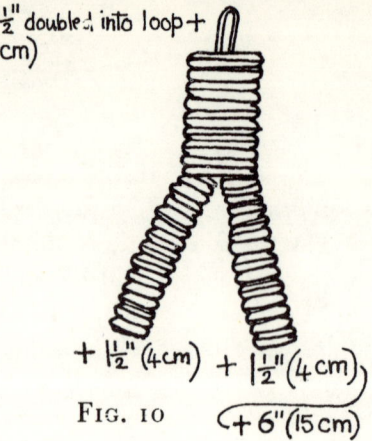

1½" doubled into loop+ (4 cm)

+ 1½" (4cm) + 1½" (4cm)

FIG. 10 (+ 6" (15 cm)

STARTING AND FINISHING ELASTIC

A. *Reinforcement circles*

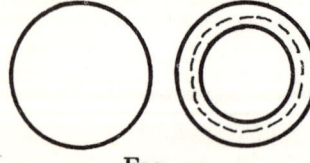

FIG. 11

Cut circle of firm cotton, tack down edge.

Cotton can be any colour as it is covered.

FIG. 12

On 1 in (*2.5 cm*) diameter circles tacking is tricky as edge will not lie flat. Use a hemming stitch folding over material as you work, even though end product is not a perfect circle.

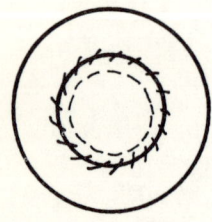

FIG. 13

Place on toy circle. Tacked down raw edge is next to toy circle. Oversew edge with single thread.

Whether sewn to gathered or smooth side of toy circle depends on effect required. Instructions are given with each toy.

18

Reinforce two circles. One for start and one for finish of elastic. Tacking thread is not removed.

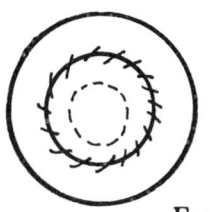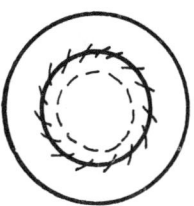

FIG. 14

B. *Stitching elastic at start*

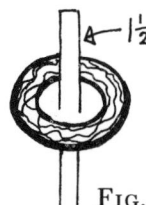

$\leftarrow 1\frac{1}{2}''(4\,cm)$ tail

Thread elastic through reinforced circle, leaving $1\frac{1}{2}$ in (*4 cm*) tail. Cotton reinforcement next to tail.
For small circles and narrow elastic leave 1 in (*2.5 cm*) tail.

FIG. 15

Take a few stitches where elastic emerges from circle. Sew through material and elastic.
This closes the tiny gap where elastic was pulled through. It also helps to take the strain.

FIG. 16

Fold tail of elastic in half. Stitch together to make a loop. Use thread double. Stitch firmly.

FIG. 17

Press down top of loop to flatten it.
There will be a loop each side of centre, like butterfly wings, lying flat on the reinforced circle.

FIG. 18

Stitch firmly right round both these loops. Stitch through elastic, reinforcement circle and both thicknesses of toy circle.

Use thread double.

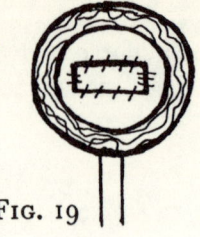

FIG. 19

C. *Stitching elastic at finish*

FIG. 20

Hold toy with elastic uppermost.

The last circle is one with cotton reinforcement with the cotton outside.

Check tension of elastic.

Push circles well down elastic, making sure there are no gaps. Elastic should be at normal, or very slightly taut, tension. If too tight it will not ping properly and great strain will be put on stitches at ends.

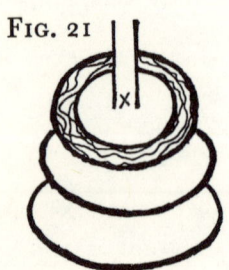

FIG. 21

Holding elastic to keep tension desired, mark it where it emerges from circles (x on diagram). White elastic—use ball pen. Black elastic—take one stitch of loose thread through elastic. This checks position so that elastic is not pulled to a different tension when sewing next stage.

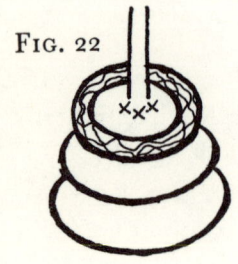

FIG. 22

Take a few stitches at marked point, sewing through material and elastic.

Cut elastic to leave tail of $1\frac{1}{2}$ in (*4 cm*).

1 in (*2·5 cm*) for small circles and narrow elastic.

Continue as Figures 17–19.

EMERGENCY DOORS

Cut circle of toy material, or of toning cotton. Tack down edge.

Circle should be large enough with edge tacked, to cover reinforcement circle.

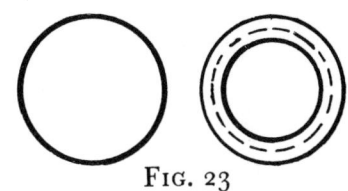

FIG. 23

Lay over elastic and reinforcement circle. Tacked down raw edge is next to toy circle. Oversew edge with single thread.

Remove tacking threads.

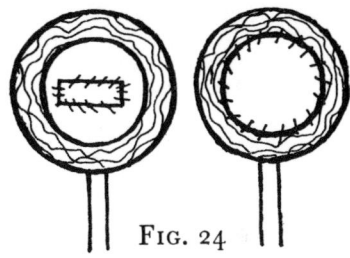

FIG. 24

Stuffed head, feet, tails, or hands, or a gathered circle can be used as emergency doors.

Ladder stitch over elastic and reinforcement circle. Use thread double. Sew round twice.

Head. Sew in place before threading on remainder of circles. It is easier to handle.

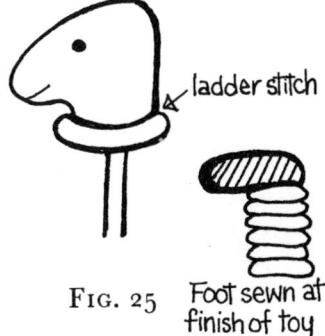

FIG. 25   Foot sewn at finish of toy

If hands etc. are too small to cover elastic and reinforcement circle, put on an emergency door as Figures 23 and 24. Then sew hand on to it.

Use double thread. Ladder stitch round twice.

FIG. 26

21

Emergency Doors allow elastic to be changed when it perishes with age or wears out.

Unpick the stitching round the emergency doors. The ends of elastic come into view and can be unstitched and cut off. The toy can be re-threaded with new elastic and the emergency doors sewn back into place.

PREPARING ARM AND LEG ELASTIC

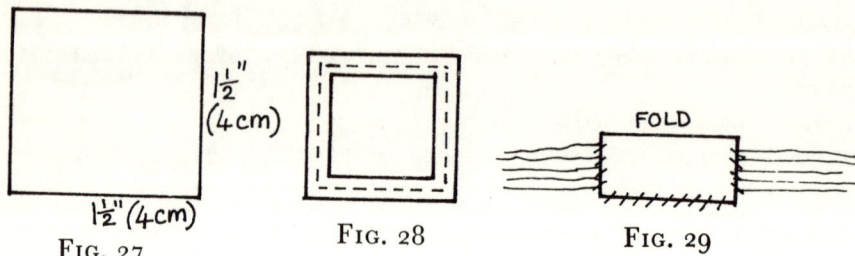

FIG. 27   FIG. 28   FIG. 29

Arm or Leg Junction: Cut piece of cotton toning with toy, 1½ in (*4 cm*) square.

Turn over edges. Tack down.

Fold in half. Sew round centre of elastic. Take two or three stitches through centre of elastic.

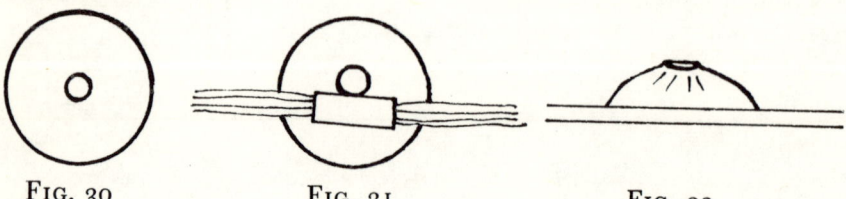

FIG. 30   FIG. 31   FIG. 32

Take one gathered body circle. Make hole for body elastic

Sew arm or leg junction close to hole. Use double thread. Sew very firmly, through junction, elastic and both thicknesses of circle.

Usually sewn on under side of body circle and on smooth side rather than gathered side, but this depends on toy.

22

Body and legs:

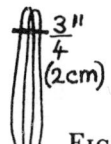

FIG. 33

Fold elastic in half. $\frac{3}{4}$ in (*2 cm*) from fold stitch both thicknesses together. Use thread double.

FIG. 34

Put elastic through top body circle with reinforcement circle uppermost. Take a few stitches where elastic emerges from circle. Sew through material and elastic.

FIG. 35

Press down top of loop to flatten it as Figure 18 (page 19).

FIG. 36

Stitch firmly right round both these loops. Stitch through elastic, reinforcement circle and both thicknesses of toy circle as Fig. 19 (page 20).

FIG. 37

Ladder stitch head on now. It acts as emergency door. Use thread double. Stitch round twice.

If head is narrow, sew on emergency door, then sew on head.

Attach head so that body elastic is facing sideways, then it will divide neatly at hips to form legs.

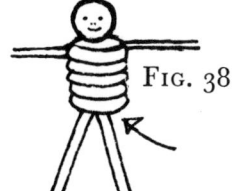

FIG. 38

Thread on body circles, including the one with the arm elastic.

At hips, stitch through both thicknesses of elastic before they separate for legs. (see arrow). Also stitch last body circle to close gap at hole where double elastic emerges, to help to take the strain.

23

Thread on leg circles, finishing with one with reinforcement circle. Finish off elastic at ends of legs as Figs. 20–2 (page 20).

Sew on emergency doors and/or feet (page 21).

FIG. 39

Thread on arm circles, finishing with one with reinforced circle.

Finish off elastic at ends of arms as Figs. 20–2 (page 20).

Sew on emergency doors and/or hands (page 21).

FIG. 40

Finish head, putting on features and hair.

FIG. 41

Hint

When threading first circle of body, which will form the shouders, thread it smooth side upwards for a boy to give smooth masculine shoulders and gathered side upwards for a girl to give a frilly look.

BOY   GIRL.

FIG. 42 FIG. 43

I. SNEAKY SNAKE

Sneaky Snake

The one in the photograph is 2 feet (*60 cm*) long and has eighty-five body circles.

It can be any length. Make head and tail, then sew any number of body circles.

For colour ideas see 'Imagination with Material', page 135.

25

MATERIALS

Green fabric, plain or patterned	*Body.* Any number of circles, diameter 5 in (*12·5 cm*).
Emerald green taffeta	*Head.* 2 pieces, each 5 in × 3½ in (*12·5 cm × 9 cm*).
	Tail. 3 circles, diameter 4 in (*10 cm*).
	2 circles, diameter 3 in (*7·5 cm*).
	Tip of Tail. 2 pieces, each 5 in × 2 in (*12·5 cm × 5 cm*).
Firm cotton, any colour	*Reinforcement Circles.* 1 circle, diameter 2 in (*5 cm*).
	1 circle, diameter 1½ in (*4 cm*).

Thread. Machine twist: emerald green and black.
Stranded cotton: red and yellow.

Filling. Plastic foam chips.

Elastic. ¼ in (*6 mm*) wide. Calculate length when body circles are sewn (page 17).

If buying material. Body: ½ yd (*45 cm*) of 36-in (*90 cm*) wide material will give 21 circles.

Emerald green taffeta for head and tail: 5 in (*12·5 cm*) of 36-in (*90 cm*) wide material.

CIRCLES Gather body and tail circles (page 16).

REINFORCEMENT CIRCLES Following page 18, attach the larger one to the gathered side of a body circle and the smaller one to smooth side of a 3-in (*7·5-cm*) diameter tail circle.

HEAD AND TIP OF TAIL

Trace patterns. Cut two pieces for head and two pieces for tip of tail.

Place wrong sides together. Backstitch ¼ in (*6 mm*) from edge, using thread single or double according to thickness of material. Leave dotted line AB open. Turn over edge round AB. Use thread double and gather round AB but do not pull up.

Turn to right side. Stuff with foam chips. Pull up gathers. Finish off thread by taking a few stitches backwards and forwards across hole to close it.

26

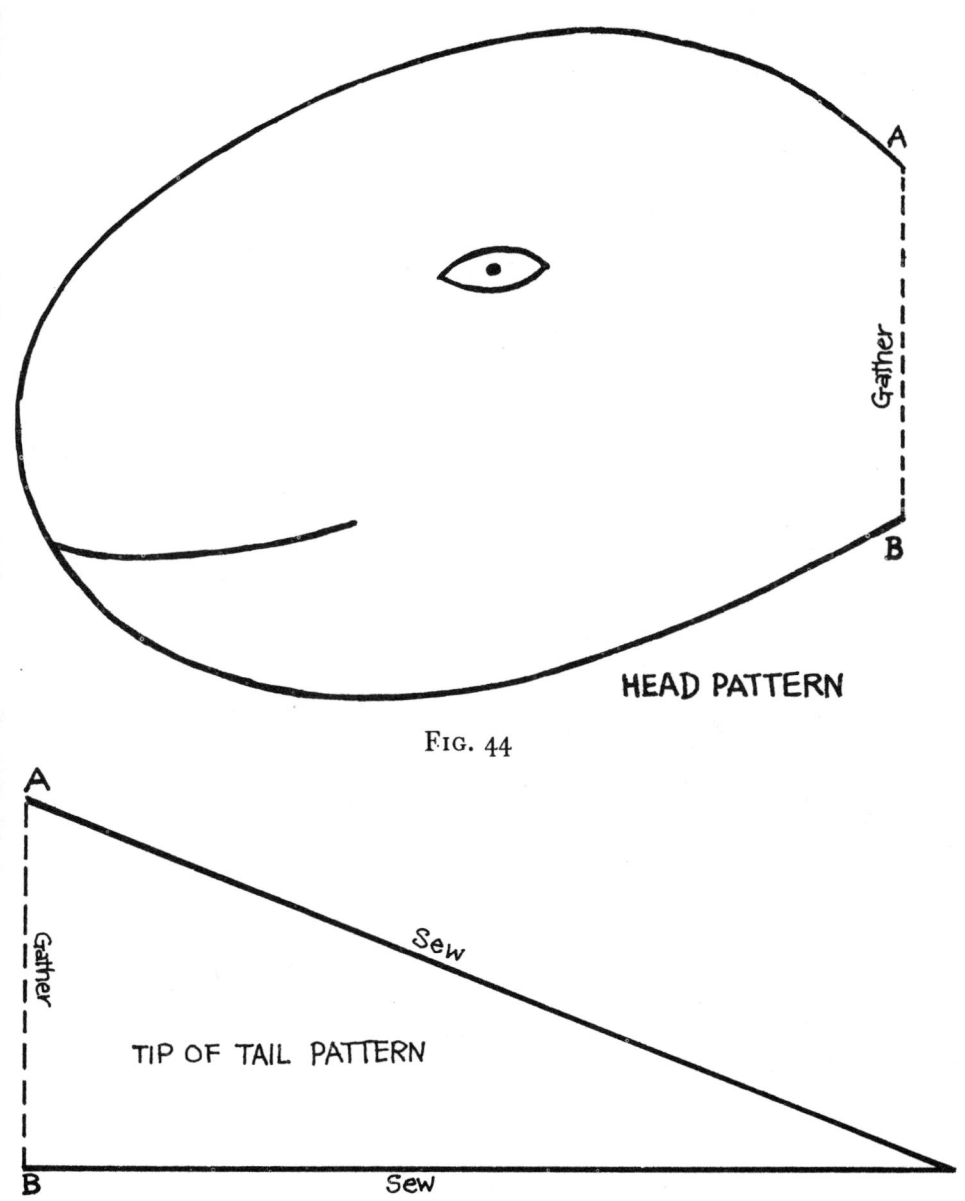

A

Gather

B

HEAD PATTERN

Fig. 44

A

Gather

Sew

TIP OF TAIL PATTERN

B Sew

Fig. 45

27

Eyes. Yellow stranded cotton: Satin stitch eye on each side. Black machine twist used double: Take a few satin stitches in the centre of eye to form pupil.

Mouth. Red stranded cotton (three strands): Stem stitch. Work along line two or three times to give a curved grin.

ASSEMBLY

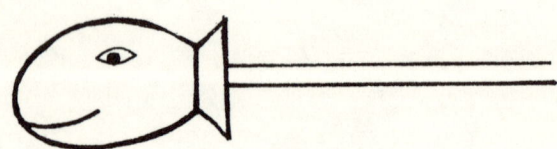

FIG. 46

Attach elastic to body circle which has reinforcement circle on it (page 19).

Emergency Door. Ladder stitch head on to cover elastic. Use thread double. Stitch round twice.

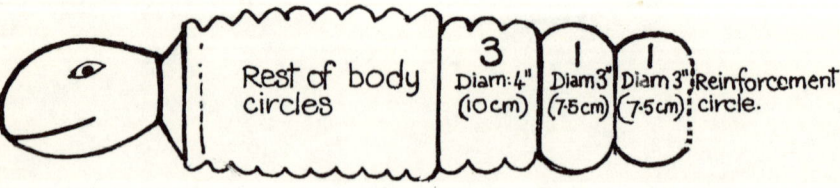

FIG. 47

Thread on rest of circles in order shown, all with gathered side towards head.

Finish off elastic (page 20).

Emergency Door. Ladder stitch tip of tail in place, covering elastic. Use thread double. Stitch round twice.

2. SAD SAM THE BASSET HOUND

Sad Sam the Basset Hound

Black and white check gingham body, black head and feet, brilliant orange ears.

MATERIALS

Check gingham, black and white	*Body.*	22 circles, diameter 5 in (*12·5 cm*).
	Legs.	4 pieces, each 3 in × 2½ in (*7·5 cm × 6·5 cm*).
	Tail.	1 piece, 5 in × 3 in (*12·5 cm × 7·5 cm*).

Black cotton	*Emergency Door.* 1 circle, diameter 2 in (*5 cm*).
Black cotton	*Head.* 2 pieces, 4¾ in × 4½ in (*12 cm × 11·5 cm*).
	Head Gusset. 1 piece, 7 in × 2½ in (*18 cm × 6·5 cm*).
	Feet. 8 circles, diameter 1½ in (*4 cm*).
	Reinforcement Circles. 1 circle, diameter 2 in (*5 cm*).
Orange cotton	*Ears.* 4 pieces, each 5½ in × 4½ in (*14 cm × 11·5 cm*).
White cotton	*Eyes.* 4 pieces, each 1½ in × 1 in (*4 cm × 2·5 cm*).
Firm cotton, any colour	*Reinforcement Circle.* 1 circle, diameter 2 in (*5 cm*).

Thread. Machine twist: Black, white and orange.

Stranded cotton (or machine twist used double): Brown and red.

Filling. Plastic foam chips.

Thin plastic foam sheeting or tweed:

Feet. 4 circles, diameter 1 in (*2·5 cm*).

If buying material. Black and white check check gingham: ½ yard (*45 cm*) of 36 in (*90 cm*) wide material (reduce body circles to 21).

Black cotton: 5 in (*12·5 cm*) of 36-in (*90-cm*) wide material (¼ yard (*23 cm*) will do three toys).

CIRCLES   Gather 22 body circles (page 16).

REINFORCEMENT CIRCLES   Following page 18, attach the black one to the gathered side of a body circle and the other one to the smooth side of another body circle.

HEAD

Trace pattern. Cut two heads in black cotton. Trace head gusset pattern on to folded paper. Cut out in black cotton. Pin one side of gusset to head, matching A and B, wrong sides to outside. With black thread, used double, backstitch this seam ¼ in (*6 mm*) from edge.

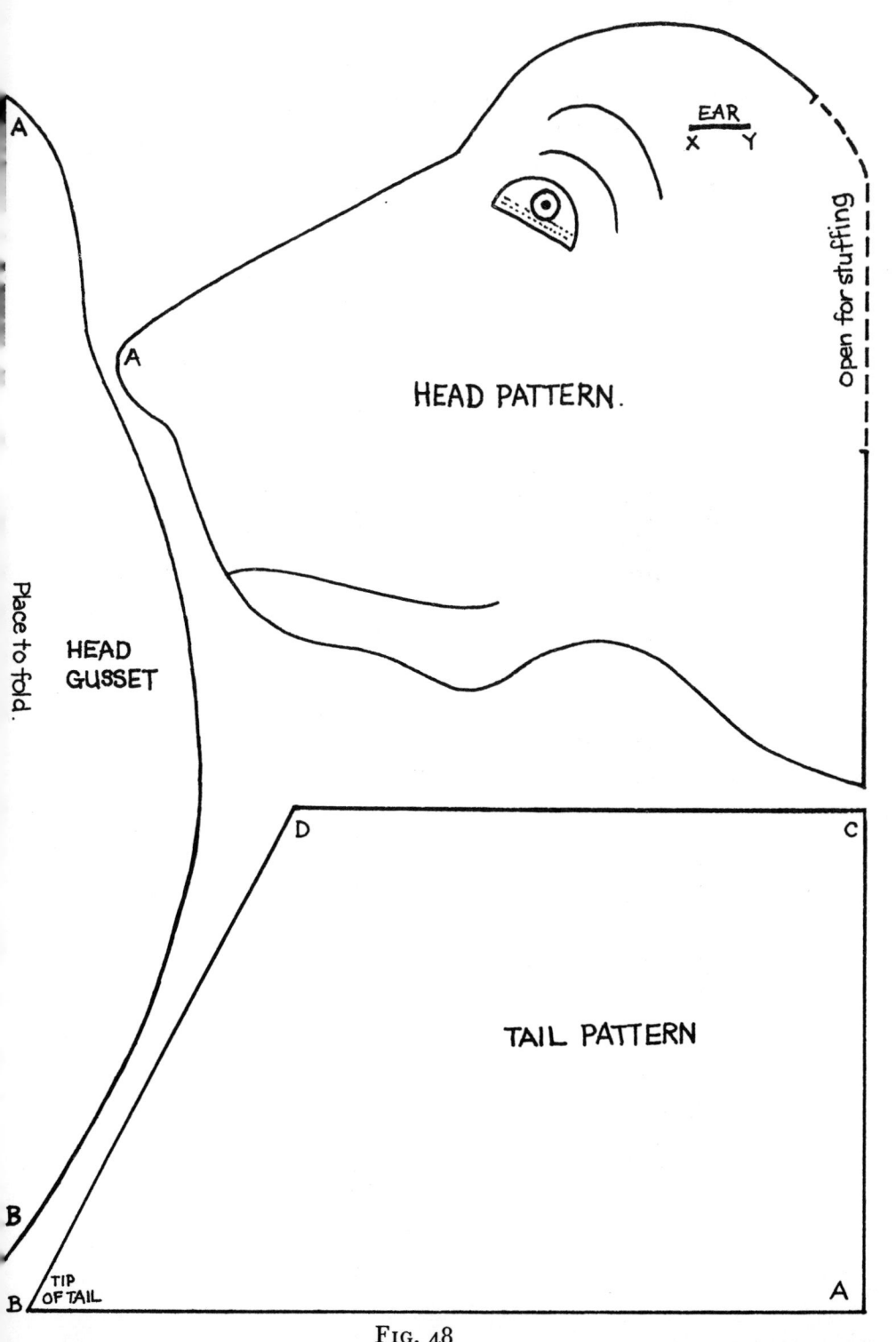

A

EAR
X Y

open for stuffing

HEAD PATTERN.

A

Place to fold.

HEAD
GUSSET

D   C

TAIL PATTERN

B

B   TIP
OF TAIL   A

Fig. 48

Backstitch second side of gusset to other head, but leave opening for stuffing at dotted line. Now backstitch remainder of two heads together from A, under chin and round to B. Turn back and tack edges round opening. Turn to right side. Stuff with foam chips. Ladder stitch to close opening.

LEGS

Speed tip. Do all four legs at once, doing the same stage on each one at the same time.

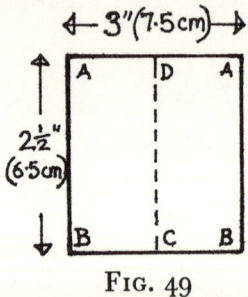

FIG. 49

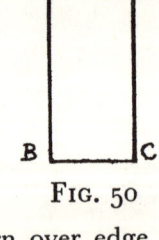

FIG. 50

Fold in half at dotted line, matching points A and B, with wrong side to outside. Using single thread, backstitch AB.

Turn over edge round AD. Tack down.

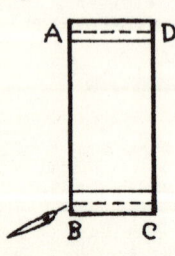

FIG. 51

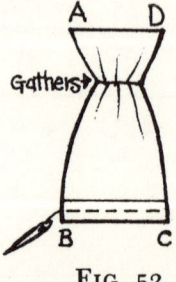

FIG. 52

FIG. 53

Turn over edge round BC. Gather, using double thread, but do not pull up. Turn to right side.

½ in (*1·5 cm*) down from AD run gathering thread round, using double thread. Pull up tight.

Stuff lower leg. Pull up gathering thread at BC. Finish off.

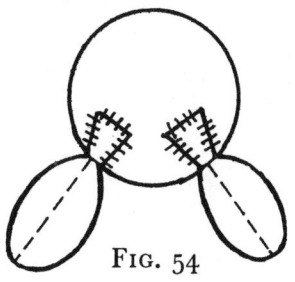

FIG. 54

Attach two legs to the smooth side of a body circle. With black thread double sew securely round the unstuffed top of each leg (Fig. 53: AD to gathers). Have legs sticking out at a slight angle, with the leg seam at centre back of leg. Sew remaining two legs to smooth side of another body circle.

FEET

Place two black circles together, wrong sides to outside. With black thread single, backstitch $\frac{1}{4}$ in (*6 mm*) from edge, a little over halfway round. Turn down and tack edge round opening. Turn right side out. Slip foam circle inside. Slipstitch across opening. Repeat with remaining circles to make four feet.

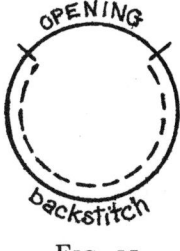

FIG. 55

Ladder stitch a foot to base of each leg. Place the sewn opening to back of leg. Use black thread double and stitch round twice.

FIG. 56

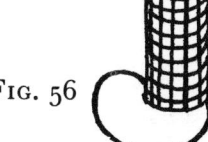

TAIL

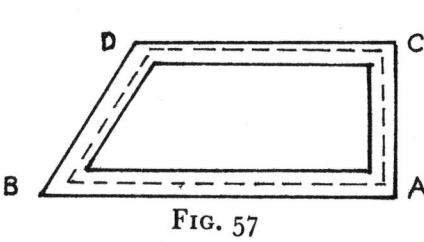

FIG. 57

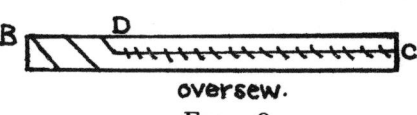

oversew.

FIG. 58

Trace pattern. Cut one piece in check. Turn down and tack raw edge all round. Use black or white thread. Make small stitches and they can be left in.

Start at side AB. Roll across tail till CD is reached. Pin along CD. Oversew tip of tail at B, using black thread single and small stitches. Then sew along D to C. Spiral between D and B does not need sewing.

33

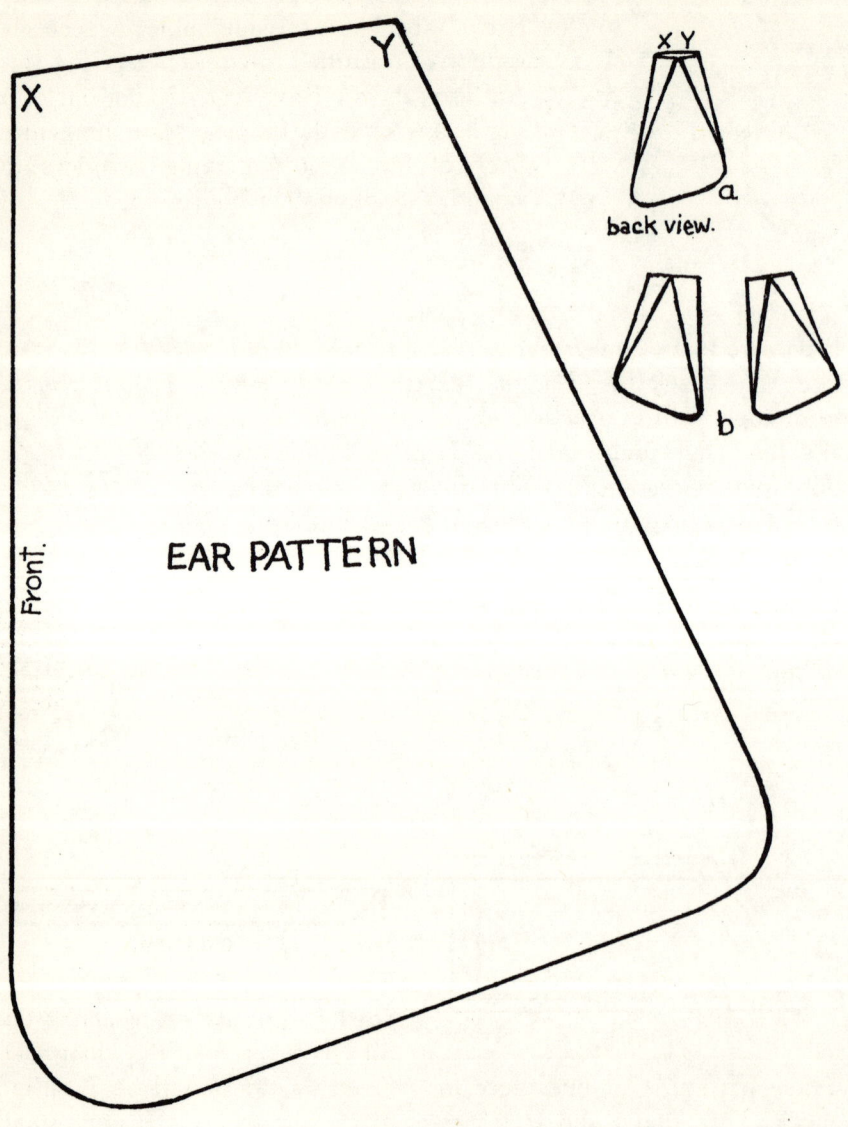

X Y

Y

X

Front.

EAR PATTERN

back view.

a

b

Fig. 59

34

Trace pattern. Cut four in orange cotton. If material has right and wrong side cut two, then reverse pattern for second two, to make two pairs.

Place two ears together, wrong sides outside. With orange thread single, backstitch ¼ in (*6 mm*) from edge, leaving top, XY, open. Turn down raw edge round top and tack. Turn right side out. Slipstitch sides together to close top. Turn corners X and Y to meet at centre back (Fig. 59a). Take a few stitches right through to hold them in place. When doing second ear, make sure corners are turned so that ears form a pair (Fig. 59b).

ASSEMBLY

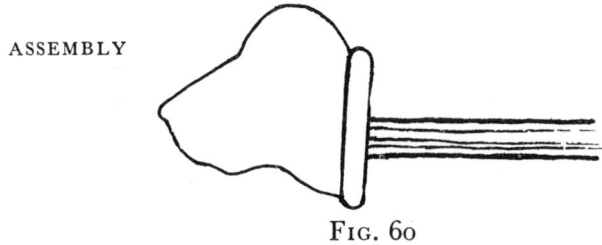

FIG. 60

Attach elastic to body circle which has black reinforcement circle on it (page 19).

Emergency door. Place head to cover elastic. Put lower point of neck to edge of black circle (see A on Fig. 60). This leaves check edge showing. Using black thread double, ladder stitch round twice where head and circle touch. Head should conceal elastic but will leave part of black reinforcement circle showing. This blends the black head on to the body.

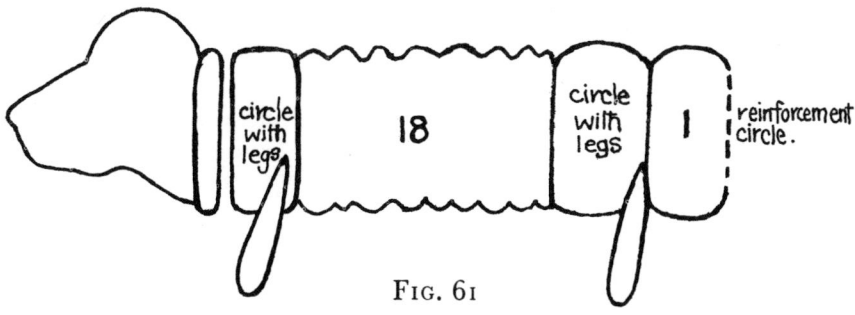

FIG. 61

Thread rest of circles in order shown, all with gathered side towards head. Finish off elastic (page 20). Sew check emergency door circle on to end of body (page 21).

(page 20). ... (page 21).

FINISHING TOUCHES

Tail. Sew tail (end marked C) to centre of emergency door. Using thread double, ladder stitch round twice.

Ears. Ladder stitch ear to each side of head along line XY (see Fig. 48). Ear is about $\frac{3}{4}$ in (*2 cm*) from top seam of head. Folded corners are between ear and head.

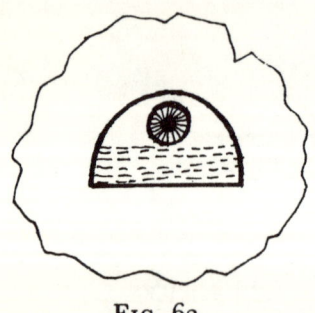

FIG. 62

Eyes. Trace pattern: Place pattern on one piece of white cotton on wrong side. Pencil round it. Lay second piece of cotton underneath and cut roughly $\frac{1}{4}$ in (*6 mm*) out from pencil line. With single white thread backstitch round curved pencil line, sewing through both thicknesses of cotton. Turn back edges on straight lines and tack down. Turn to right side. Slip-stitch along straight edges to close gap.

Embroider brown satin stitch circle for iris as shown on diagram (two strands of stranded cotton or brown machine twist used double). Sew black pupil on top of it. Along bottom of eye put three or four rows of running stitch in red to represent bloodshot eyes. Stagger the stitches. Repeat for second eye.

Sew an eye to each side of head (position shown on head diagram). Use black thread double and sew round twice.

Wrinkles. Embroider two above each eye with brown thread and stem stitch (shown on head diagram).

Mouth. Embroider, in stem stitch, with red stranded cotton, two strands. Keep•the line drooping a little from the centre nose seam to give the dog a sad look, which is typical of basset hounds.

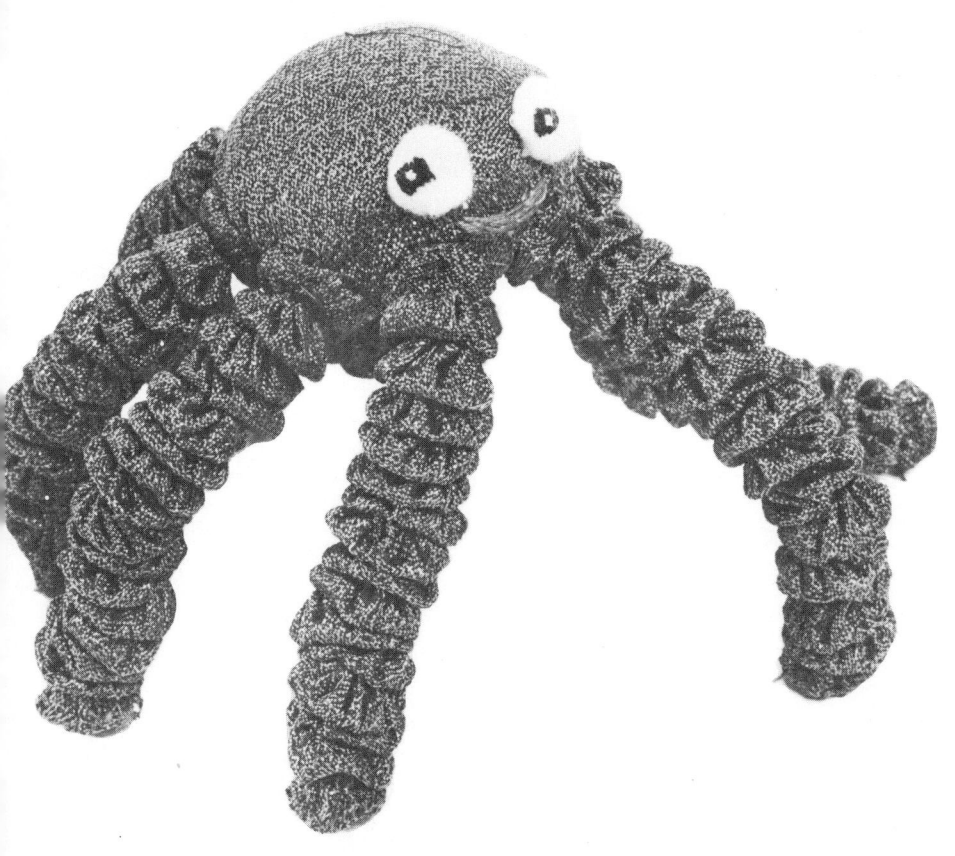

3. WAVY-LEGS THE OCTOPUS

Wavy-Legs the Octopus

Most effective in emerald green shimmering material, with touches of lurex thread in it, such as cuttings from an evening dress.

37

Emerald green silk   *Legs.*   128 circles, diameter 2 in (*5 cm*) (8 legs of 16 circles each). As different thickness of material can alter length make circles for one leg, thread on cotton and measure. Leg should be about 4 in (*10 cm*) long.

                             Body.   1 circle diameter 6 in (*15 cm*).

                             Body Base. 1 circle, diameter 2 in (*5 cm*) approximately, but do not cut till body is made.

                             Emergency Doors. 8 circles, diameter 1 in (*2·5 cm*).

Yellow fabric   *Eyes.*   2 circles, diameter 1½ in (*4 cm*).

Firm cotton,   *Reinforcement circles.* 16 circles, diameter 1 in (*2·5 cm*).
  any colour

Oddment of anything: 1 circle diameter 2 in (*5 cm*).

Thread. Machine twist: emerald green and yellow.
             Standed cotton: red and black.

Filling. Plastic foam chips.

Elastic. 8 pieces of 8 in (*20·5 cm*) each. ⅟₁₆ in (*5 mm*) wide.

If buying material. ½ yard (*45 cm*) of 36-in (*90 cm*) wide material.

CIRCLES   Gather 128 leg circles (page 16).

REINFORCEMENT CIRCLES   Following page 18, attach one each to the gathered side of 8 leg circles, and one each to the smooth side of 8 leg circles.

BODY

Turn edge to wrong side. Gather, using thread double.

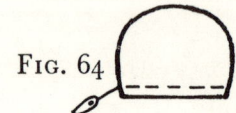

FIG. 63

Start pulling up gathers, so that right side is to outside. Stuff with foam chips. Pull up a little more, adding more foam to get a fairly firm circle.   FIG. 64

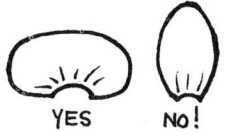

Keep centre of circle flat to make top of head.

FIG. 66

Add bits of stuffing just inside gathers to get a firm edging for attaching the legs (see arrows on diagram).

Pull up as tightly as possible. Finish off thread, stitching backwards and forwards across hole.

Cover hole in base of body. The size of the hole can vary according to the stiffness of the material, and the amount of stuffing used. Experiment with the oddment circle: tack down edge and pin across hole. If it does not cover it cut a bigger circle and try again. When correct, use as pattern to cut the body base circle in green material. Tack down edge, pin across hole and ladder stitch round twice, using thread double.

EYES

BACK
Gathers at centre

FLAT FRONT
Eye embroidered

FIG. 67

On each yellow circle, fold over edge, and gather, using thread double. Pull up tight and stitch across gathers to finish off thread. Press flat. Use black stranded cotton to embroider a satin stitch eye. Put it to one side, rather than in the centre.

Use the yellow machine twist single to take a few stitches in centre of black eye.

ASSEMBLY

Attach the 8 lengths of elastic to the 8 leg circles that have reinforcement circles on the gathered side (page 19).

Fig. 68

Fig 69

Place pins round body to mark position for legs. Pin just below widest bit of bulge.

Ladder stitch each leg to body. Using thread double, stitch round twice.

On to each leg thread another 14 circles, gathered side towards body. Then thread on circle that has reinforcement circle on smooth side. Finish off elastic (page 20).

Sew 1 in (*2·5 cm*) green emergency door circle to end of each leg to cover elastic (page 21).

FINISHING TOUCHES

Fig. 70

Eyes. Ladder stitch to head, using green thread double. Stitch round twice. Sew on edge of bulge, each above a leg so that a space is left between legs for mouth.

Mouth. Red stranded cotton (four strands). Use stem stitch, sewing along two or three times, to give a curved smile.

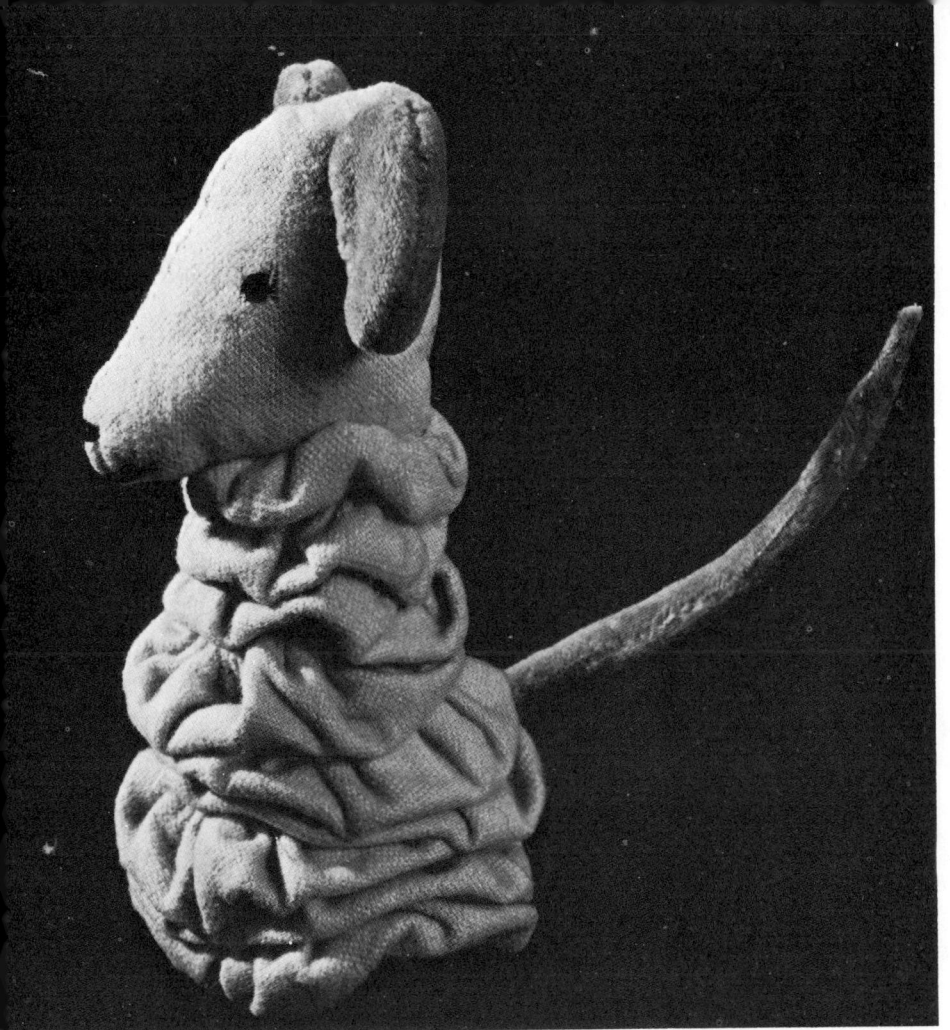

4. DINKIE MOUSE

Dinkie Mouse

Blue winceyette head and body with ears and tail in pink velvet.

MATERIALS

Blue winceyette   *Body.*   9 circles, one each of diameter 6 in, $5\frac{3}{4}$, $5\frac{1}{2}$, $5\frac{1}{4}$, 5, $4\frac{3}{4}$, $4\frac{1}{2}$, $4\frac{1}{4}$ and 4 in (*15 cm, 14·5, 14, 13·5, 12·5, 12, 11·5, 11, 10 cm*).

                      Head.   2 pieces each $3\frac{1}{4}$ in × 3 in (*8·5 cm × 7·5 cm*).

                      Emergency Door. 1 circle, diameter 2 in (*5 cm*).

Pink velvet   *Ears.*   4 pieces each 2 in × $1\frac{1}{2}$ in (*5 cm × 4 cm*).

                      Tail.   1 piece, 6 in × 1 in (*15 cm × 2·5 cm*).

Firm cotton· *Reinforcement Circles.* 1 circle, diameter 2 in (*5 cm*).
  any colour   1 circle, diameter $1\frac{1}{2}$ in (*4 cm*).

Thread. Machine twist: blue, pink and black (or black stranded cotton).

Copydex. For sticking tail.

Filling. Plastic foam chips.

Elastic. $9\frac{1}{2}$ in (*24 cm*), $\frac{3}{16}$ in (*5 mm*) wide.

If buying material. $\frac{1}{2}$ yard (*45 cm*) of 36-in (*90-cm*) wide material will easily make two mice. $\frac{1}{4}$ yard (*23 cm*) might just do one if you are clever at juggling patterns (this short length gives unavoidable wastage beside some circles) or miss out one of the bigger body circles.

CIRCLES   Gather the 9 body circles (page 16).

Pin a slip of paper, with diameter size marked on it, to each one as it is cut and sewn so that it is easy to thread them together in the correct order.

REINFORCEMENT CIRCLES   Following page 18, attach the $1\frac{1}{2}$ in (*4 cm,* diameter one to the gathered side of the 4 in (*10 cm*) diameter body circle. Attach the 2 in (*5 cm*) diameter one to the smooth side of the 6 in (*15 cm*) diameter body circle.

HEAD and EARS

Trace patterns. Cut two pieces for head in blue winceyette. If material has wrong side turn pattern over before cutting second piece to make a

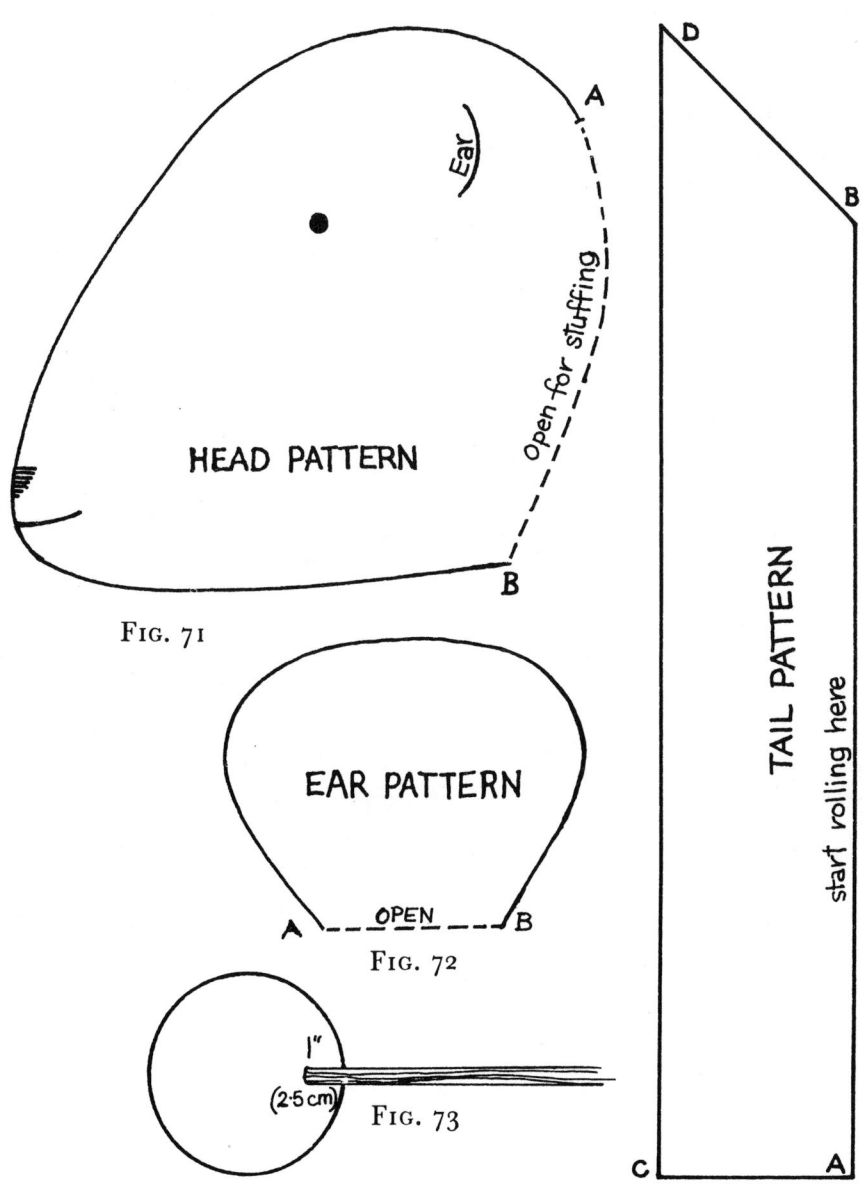

HEAD PATTERN

Ear

Open for stuffing

A

B

FIG. 71

EAR PATTERN

OPEN

A   B

FIG. 72

1"

(2·5 cm)   FIG. 73

TAIL PATTERN

start rolling here

D

B

C   A

pair. Cut four pieces for ears in pink velvet. Place two heads together, two ears and two ears, all wrong side to outside. Use thread double and backstitch together, $\frac{1}{4}$ in (*6 mm*) from the edge, leaving opening from A to B as shown dotted on diagram. Turn over raw edges round openings and tack down. Turn to right side. Stuff head with foam chips (not ears). Ladder stitch along opening on head and ears.

Use blue thread double and ladder stitch one ear to each side of head. Position shown by line on head diagram. Stitch round twice.

TAIL

Trace pattern. Cut one piece in pink velvet. Cover wrong side lightly with Copydex. Roll up tail, starting at AB and rolling up to side CD. Now roll tail between fingers and palms. This will help to form a neat rolled shape, especially at the pointed tip.

Lay unpointed end (AC) on smooth side of the $5\frac{3}{4}$ in (*14·5 cm*) diameter circle. Overlap it for about 1 in (*2·5 cm*). Use blue thread double and ladder stitch round it, stitching round twice.

ASSEMBLY

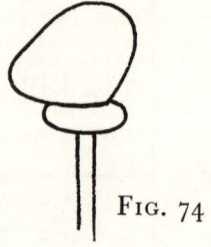

FIG. 74

Attach elastic to the 4 in (*10 cm*) diameter body circle which has the reinforcement circle on it (page 19).

Emergency Door. Ladder stitch head on to circle to cover elastic. Using thread double, stitch round twice.

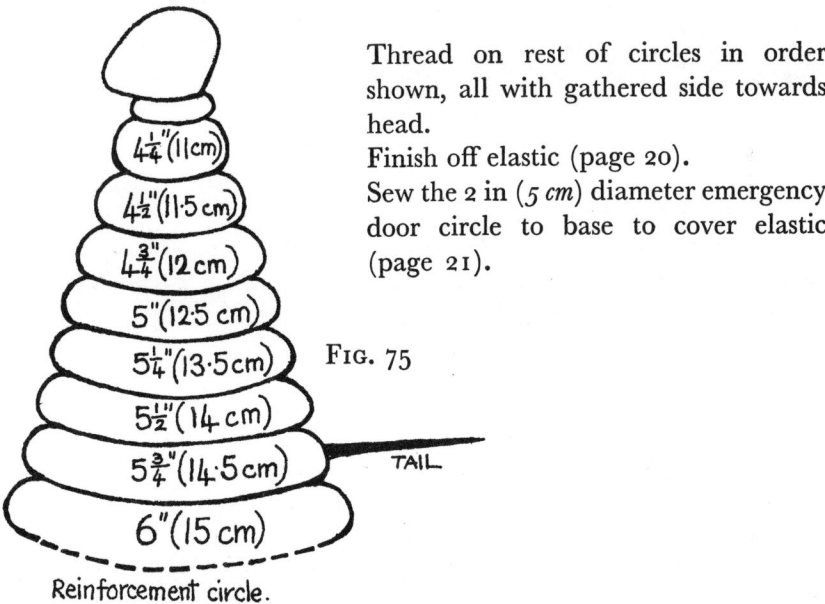

Thread on rest of circles in order shown, all with gathered side towards head.

Finish off elastic (page 20).

Sew the 2 in (*5 cm*) diameter emergency door circle to base to cover elastic (page 21).

FIG. 75

$4\frac{1}{4}$"(11cm)

$4\frac{1}{2}$"(11·5 cm)

$4\frac{3}{4}$"(12 cm)

5"(12·5 cm)

$5\frac{1}{4}$"(13·5cm)

$5\frac{1}{2}$"(14 cm)

$5\frac{3}{4}$"(14·5cm)   TAIL

6"(15 cm)

Reinforcement circle.

FEATURES

FIG. 76

Position shown in head diagram. Use black thread double. Embroider a satin stitch eye each side. Use stem stitch to mark nose and mouth.

45

Ugglie, a Caveman

No stuffiing required.

Swarthy orange head with patterned brown cotton body to represent his animal skin clothes. Features are felt, so put a little salt in the water when washing to help to prevent colours running.

MATERIALS

Orange cotton	*Head.*	6 circles, diameter 6 in (*15 cm*).
(duster cloth is		1 circle, diameter 5 in (*12·5 cm*).
very effective)		1 circle, diameter 4½ in (*11·5 cm*).
Patterened brown	*Body.*	12 circles, diameter 6 in (*15 cm*).
cotton or cottons	*Emergency Door.*	1 circle, diameter 2 in (*5 cm*).
in different browns		
Firm cotton,	*Lining circle.*	1 circle, diameter 2 in (*5 cm*).
dark colour		
Firm cotton,	*Reinforcement Circles.*	2 circles, diameter 2 in (*5 cm*).
any colour		
Felt	*Features.*	Scraps of red, white, blue and yellow.
Black wool	*Hair.*	Thick wool, 12½ yards (*10·5 metres*).

Thread. Machine twist: orange, brown, black, white and red.

Copydex. For sticking features.

Ball pen. Black.

Elastic. 11 in (*28 cm*), ¼ in (*6 mm*) wide.

If buying material. Orange: 24 in × 18 in (*60 cm × 45 cm*).

Patterned brown: 12 in (*30 cm*) of 36-in (*90-cm*) wide material

CIRCLES Gather all the orange circles and 11 brown body circles (page 16). Gather the twelfth brown body circle, but, before pulling up gathers, slip the lining circle inside it.

REINFORCEMENT CIRCLES Following page 18, attach one to smooth

46

5. UGGLIE, A CAVEMAN

side of the orange circle which has diameter of 5 in (*12·5 cm*) and one to smooth side of the brown circle which has the lining circle in it.

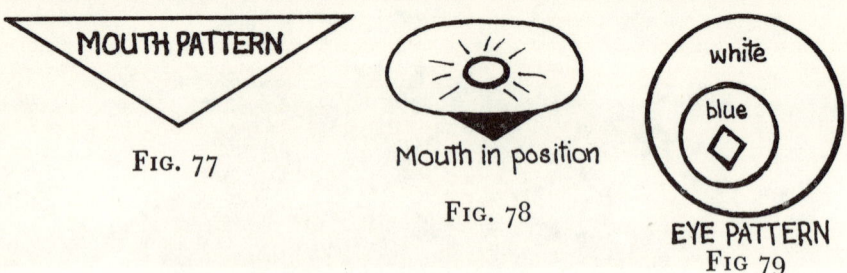

FIG. 77

Mouth in position

FIG. 78

EYE PATTERN
FIG 79

MOUTH   Trace pattern. Cut one piece in red felt. Use red thread single. Slip stitch mouth to edge of an orange circle, diameter 6 in (*15 cm*). Gathered side of circle is uppermost.

EYES   Trace pattern. Cut two large circles in white felt, two smaller circles in blue felt and two tiny diamonds in yellow felt. Use Copydex to stick yellow diamond to blue circle, then blue circle to white. Put dot in centre of yellow diamond with ball pen.

ASSEMBLY

Attach the elastic to the 5 in (*12·5 cm*) diameter orange circle which has the reinforcement circle on it (page 19).

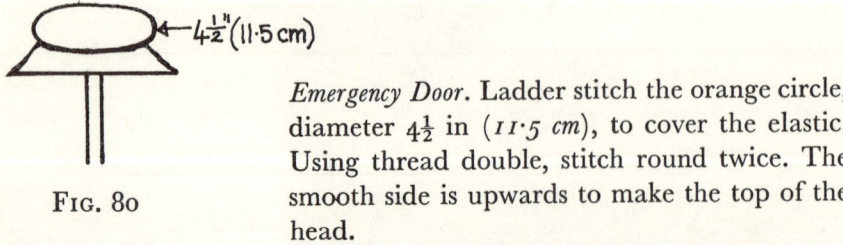

FIG. 80

Emergency Door. Ladder stitch the orange circle, diameter 4½ in (*11·5 cm*), to cover the elastic. Using thread double, stitch round twice. The smooth side is upwards to make the top of the head.

Thread on rest of circles in order shown (Fig. 81), all with gathered side towards head.

Finish off elastic (page 20).
Attach brown emergency door circle, diameter 2 in (*5 cm*), to cover elastic (page 21).

48

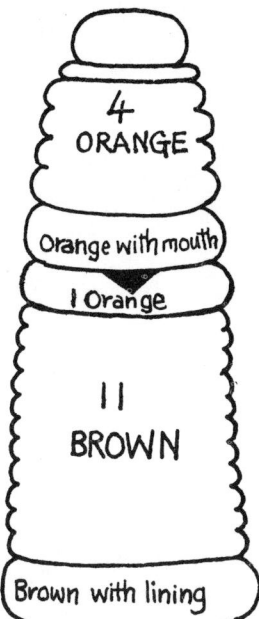

Reinforcement circle.

FIG. 81

EYES

Leaving one circle above mouth, sew eyes across the edges of the next three circles. Using white thread single, slipstitch round outer edge, catching orange base wherever it touches.

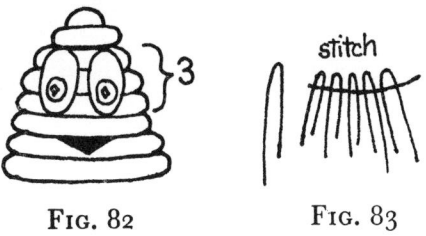

FIG. 82   FIG. 83

HAIR

Method. Fold lengths of wool roughly in half: an uneven effect is wanted (Fig. 83). Use black thread double and sew fold to fabric, putting needle right through centre of wool. Sew the folded pieces of wool next to each other, working right across section. Wool can be taken one or two pieces at a time to give varied thickness. Final effect should be an unruly mop of hair.

Lower Fringe. 16 bits of wool, 1½ in (*4 cm*) long. Sew to circle above eyes. Stitch just over top of rim.

Upper Fringe. 16 bits of wool, 5 in (*12·5 cm*) long. Sew straight across middle of top circle so that ends fall over lower fringe.

Main Hair, Lower. 24 bits of wool, 4 in (*10 cm*) long. Sew to third top circle round the back. Vary position from edge of rim to top of circle near the middle.

Main Hair, Middle. 24 bits of wool, 4 in (*10 cm*) long. Sew to second top circle round the back.

Main Hair, Upper. 24 bits of wool, 6 in (*15 cm*) long. Sew straight across middle of top circle, to meet the fringe, but so that the hair falls to the back.

49

Wee Willie Winkie

Striped winceyette for his nightshirt and nightcap with pink winceyette for head, hands and feet.

MATERIALS

Striped winceyette	*Body.*	16 circles, diameter 5 in (*12·5 cm*).
	Arms.	16 circles, diameter 2 in (*5 cm*) (8 for each arm).
	Nightcap.	1 piece, 5½ in × 5 in (*14 cm × 12·5 cm*).
	Emergency Doors.	2 circles, diameter 1 in (*2·5 cm*) for arms. 1 circle, diameter 2 in (*5 cm*). (This last circle is for base of body. For best effect do not cut it until toy is made. Then it can be cut so that stripes will match stripes on body circle and it will be practically invisible).
Pink winceyette	*Head.*	2 circles, diameter 3 in (*7·5 cm*).
	Neck.	1 circle, diameter 3 in (*7·5 cm*).
	Feet.	4 pieces, each 2½ in × 1¼ in (*6·5 cm × 3 cm*).
	Hands.	2 pieces, each 2¼ in × 1¾ in (*6 cm × 4·5 cm*).
	Ears.	4 pieces, each 1¼ in × 1 in (*3 cm × 2·5 cm*).
Firm cotton to match winceyette	*Arm junction.*	1 piece, 1½ in (*4 cm*) square.
Firm cotton, any colour	*Reinforcement Circles.*	2 circles, diameter 1½ in (*4 cm*). 2 circles, diameter 1 in (*2·5 cm*).

Wool, Small balls: red for tassel of nightcap and brown for hair.

Thread. Machine twist: white (or to match winceyette) and pink.

Stranded cotton: red, blue and black.

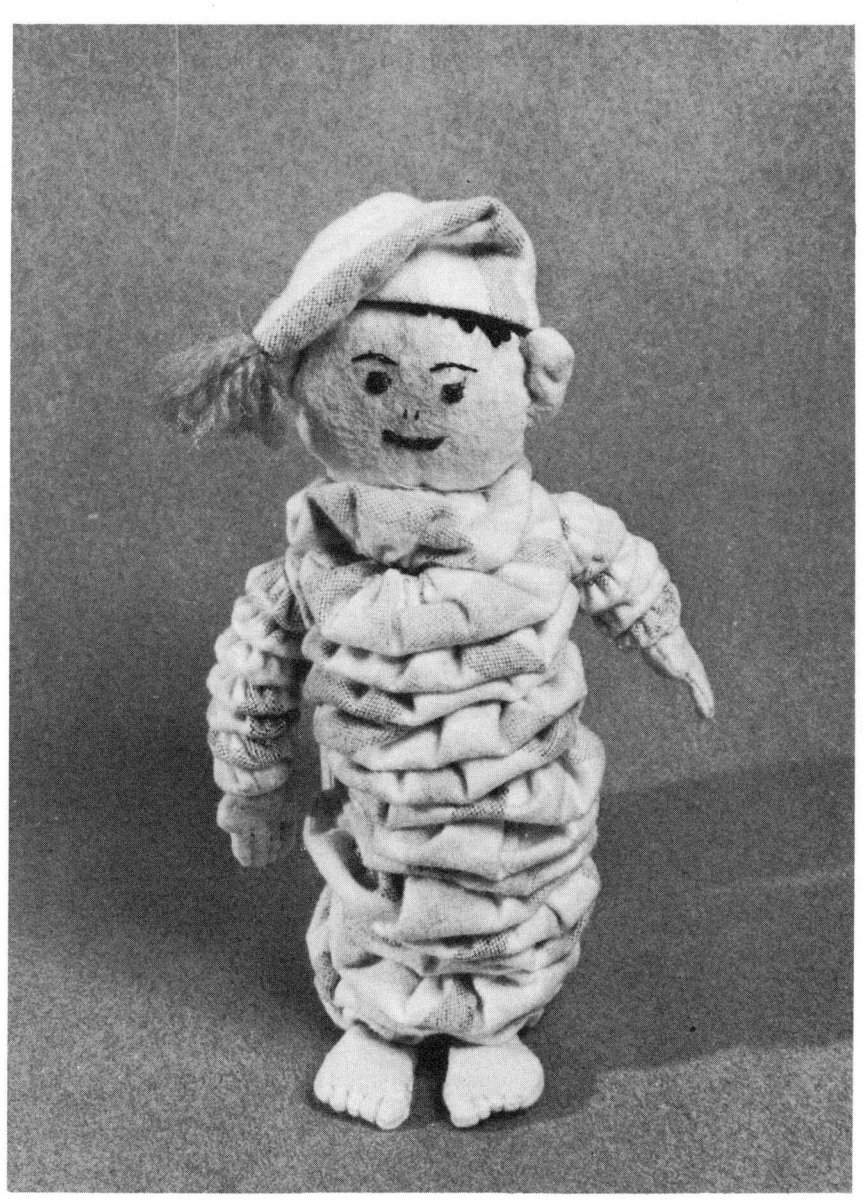

6. WEE WILLIE WINKIE

Filling. Plastic foam chips.

Thin plastic foam sheeting or tweed:
Feet.   2 pieces each 1½ in × ½ in (*4 cm* × *1·5 cm*).
Hands. 2 pieces each ¾ in × ½ in (*2 cm* × *1·5 cm*).
Elastic. Body: 11 in (*28 cm*), ¼ in (*6 mm*) wide. Arms: 12 in (*30 cm*),
        {5/16} in (*5 mm*) wide.
If buying material.   Striped winceyette: ½ yard (*45 cm*), 36 in (*90 cm*)
        wide.

CIRCLES   Gather the 16 body circles and 16 arm circles and the neck circle (page 16).

REINFORCEMENT CIRCLES   Following page 18, attach the two bigger ones to the smooth sides of two body circles and the two smaller ones to the smooth sides of two arm circles.

HEAD

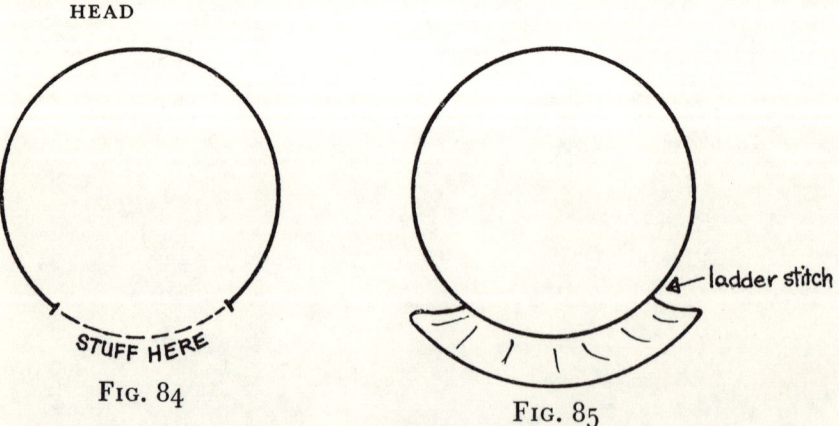

STUFF HERE

FIG. 84

ladder stitch

FIG. 85

Place the two head circles together, wrong sides to outside. Use thread double to backstitch, ¼ in (*6 mm*) from the edge. Leave opening for stuffing. Turn back raw edges round opening and tack down. Turn right side out. Stuff with foam chips, but keep surface fairly flat. Do not stuff out to get a ball shape. Ladder stitch across opening.

Place head on gathered side of the pink neck circle. Ladder stitch round twice, with pink thread used double. Occasionally take a stitch right through to smooth side of neck circle to keep it from pulling apart.

FIG. 86

Trace pattern. Cut two in pink winceyette.

FIG. 87

On each piece turn up raw edge at wrist. Use pink thread double to run gathering thread round wrist. Do not pull up.

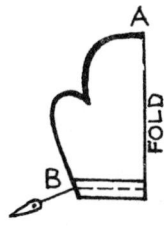

FIG. 88

Fold in half wrong side to outside. Backstitch (thread single) from A to B. $\frac{1}{4}$ in (6 mm) from edge. Turn to right side.

FIG. 89

Slip the piece of foam sheeting or tweed inside hand. Pull up gathers. Finish off hand by stitching through wrist.

FIG. 90

Fingers. Backstitch three lines with pink thread used single. Sew through all thicknesses.

FEET AND EARS

1. Trace patterns on page 54.
2. Cut four in pink winceyette for ears and four for feet. If material has a right and wrong side turn pattern over to cut two of the shapes (Fig. 93).

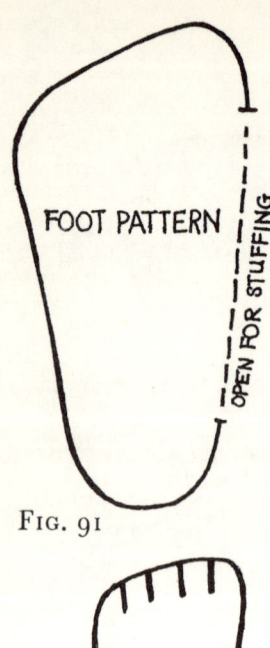

FOOT PATTERN

OPEN FOR STUFFING

FIG. 91

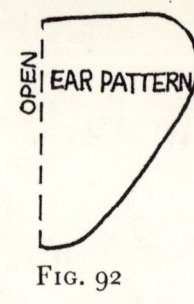

OPEN | EAR PATTERN

FIG. 92

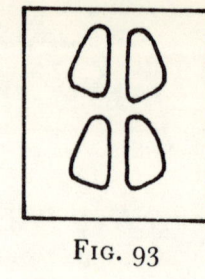

FIG. 93

FIG. 94

3. Place two pieces together, wrong sides to outside. Backstitch, with thread used single, $\frac{1}{4}$ in (*6 mm*) from edge. Leave opening in side as shown on diagram.

4. Turn back raw edge round hole. Tack down. Turn to right side.

5. Feet: Slip the piece of tweed or foam inside feet.

6. Feet and Ears: Ladder stitch across opening.

7. Toes: Mark with pink thread used single (Fig. 94).

Take three stitches for each mark, going from front of foot over top, down back and through to front again. Keep stitches fairly short.

ASSEMBLY

1. Prepare arm elastic (page 22) and sew to smooth side of a body circle (Fig. 95a).

2. Attach body elastic to a body circle with reinforcement circle on it (page 19).

3. Sew head and neck piece to cover elastic and reinforcement circle. Ladder stitch, with pink thread used double (Fig. 95b).

4. Test: Pull elastic. If neck extends as Figure 95c take a few stitches to hold it in place: take needle from underside of body circle, beside elastic, to top of neck going diagonally through a bit of the head, holding all circles together while doing so. Arrows on Figure 95d show line of stitches.

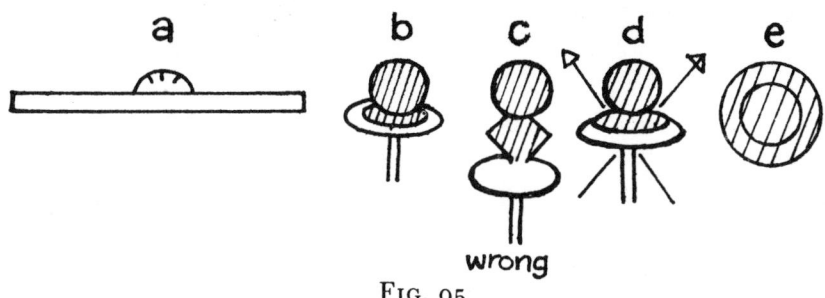

wrong

FIG. 95

5. Thread circles in order shown in Figure 96, all gathered side towards head. Do body, then arms.

6. Figure 95e shows neat effect when emergency door circle is cut so that stripes match.

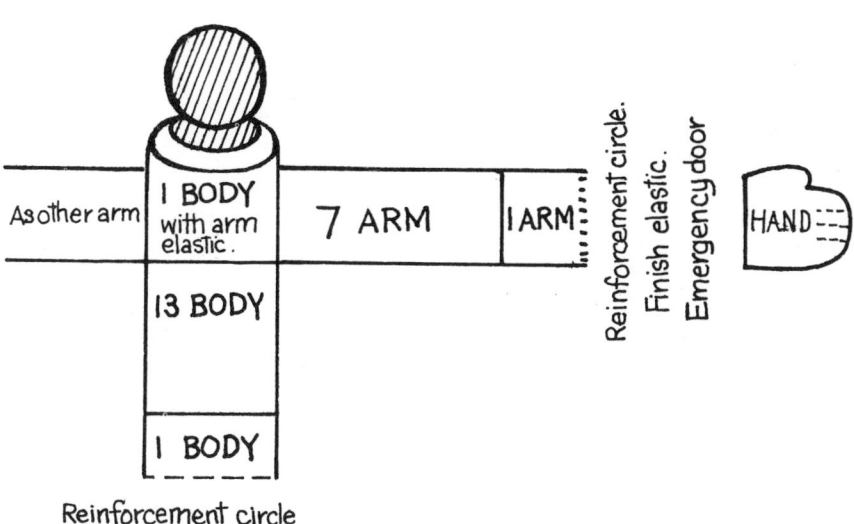

FIG. 96

Feet

Ladder stitch feet to emergency door at base of body. Place feet parallel with big toes practically touching. With pink thread used double sew twice round heel at back and across front of foot where it touches edge of emergency door. Do not sew front of foot to body circle. It is more effective if edge of body is loose like folds at end of nightshirt.

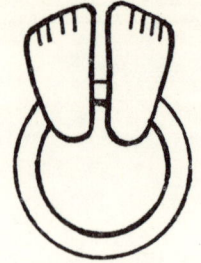

FIG. 97

Ears and Hair

FIG. 98	Back of Hair FIG. 99	Stitches FIG. 100

Ladder stitch an ear to each side of head, using thread double. Place the straight edge of the ear on side seam about half way down. Sew twice round.

Using the wool double, in a darning needle, make large stitches all over head. Choose a parting and slant stitches from it. Keep stitches wide apart at first to get shape of hair then fill in the gaps. Easiest and most economical way to stitch hair is to take one stitch, then just slip needle under a small bit of fabric, take another stitch back and so on. Diagram shows dotted lines where wool is under fabric giving large stitches for hair with very little wasted between stitches.

Features (Shown on hair diagram)

Eyes: Blue stranded cotton (three strands). Satin stitch eye. Black stranded cotton (single strand). Stem stitch eyebrows and take a few stitches in centre of blue eye.

56

Mouth: Red stranded cotton (two strands). Stem stitch curved mouth. Two small straight sitches make nostrils.

Trace pattern.

Place on folded piece of striped winceyette, wrong side to outside, and cut out.

Backstitch BC, with single thread, $\frac{1}{4}$ in (*6 mm*) from edge. Turn up a narrow hem round BD and hem with small stitches.

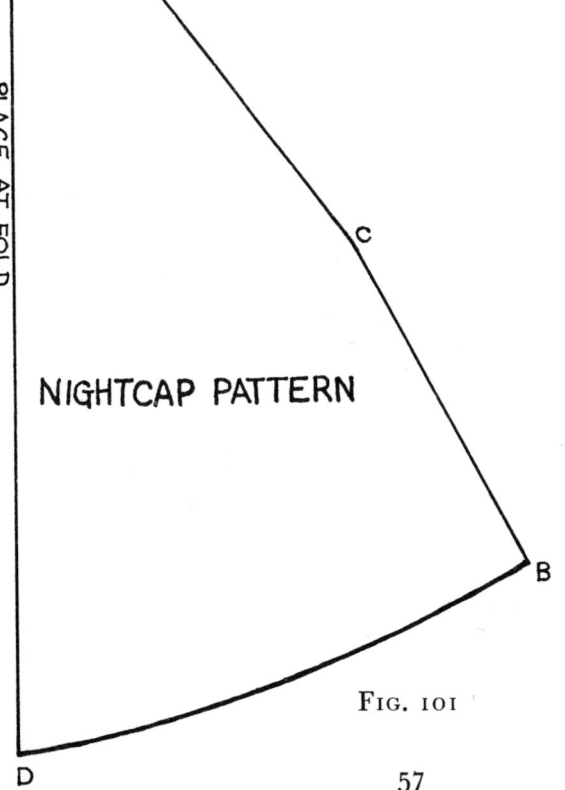

NIGHTCAP PATTERN

Fig. 101

57

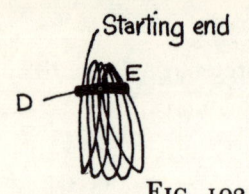

Starting end

FIG. 102

Tassel: Wind the red wool six times round three fingers, leaving the starting end hanging out. Slip off fingers. Wind working end four times round end of tassel E, then cut, leaving a tail of 3 or 4 in (*8–10 cm*) (D on diagram). Knot starting end and D tightly.

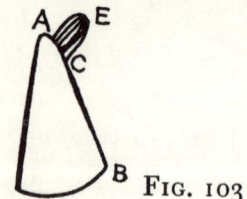

FIG. 103

Slip tassel down inside top of hat, AC, so that bound end, E, is left sticking out of hole. Backstitch firmly from A to C through tassel.

FIG. 104

Turn cap right side out. Cut ends of wool neatly.

FIG. 105

Place cap on head, the seam to centre back.

FIG. 106

Fold cap to one side. Catch points X together with ladder stitch to hold cap at this angle.
Cap may be left loose. For a baby stitch it to the head.

58

Santa Claus

Red brushed nylon for body and hood with white acrilan fur trimmings.

MATERIALS

	Number of circles	Diameter	
		in	cm
Red brushed nylon *Body.* 17 circles:	3	6	15
	3	$5\frac{3}{4}$	14.5
	2	$5\frac{1}{2}$	14
	2	$5\frac{1}{4}$	13.5
	2	5	12.5
	2	$4\frac{3}{4}$	12
	1	$4\frac{1}{2}$	11.5
	2	$4\frac{1}{4}$	11

Arms. 1 piece, 10 in × $1\frac{1}{2}$ in (*25.5 cm × 4 cm*).

Hood. 1 piece, $6\frac{1}{2}$ in × $2\frac{1}{2}$ in (*16.5 cm × 6.5 cm*).

Emergency Door. 1 circle, diameter 3 in. (*7.5 cm*).

For stuffing hands. 2 oddments, approximately 2in (*5 cm*) square.

White acrilan fur fabric *Body.* 1 circle, diameter 4 in (*10 cm*).

1 circle, diameter 6 in (*15 cm*).

Wrists. 2 pieces, each $1\frac{3}{4}$ in × $\frac{1}{2}$ in (*4.5 cm × 1.5 cm*).

Hood Trimming. 1 piece, 6 in × $\frac{1}{4}$ in (*15 cm × 6 mm*).

Measure the $\frac{1}{4}$ in (*6 mm*) generously.

Pink cotton *Head.* 2 pieces, each $3\frac{1}{4}$ in × 3 in (*8.5 cm × 7.5 cm*). Use double material if flimsy.

Hands. 2 pieces, each 2 in × $1\frac{1}{4}$ in (*5 cm × 3 cm*).

59

7. SANTA CLAUS

Firm cotton,   *Reinforcement Circles.* 2 circles, diameter 2 in (*5 cm*).
  any colour
Animal Wool. For beard, eyebrows, moustache and hair.
          Animal wool is sold in chemists' shops for chiropody.
          Alternatives: Sheep's wool found on fences, taken home
          and washed. White wool unravelled to make it single
          ply.
Thread. Machine twist: red, white and pink.
          Stranded cotton: Blue, black and red.
Copydex. For sticking animal wool.
Filling. Plastic foam chips.
Elastic. Arms: 6 in (*15 cm*) (1 piece). Body: 10½ in (*26·5 cm*). Both ¼ in
          (*6 mm*) wide.
If buying material. ½ yard (*45 cm*) of 36-in (*90-cm*) wide red material.

CIRCLES   Gather the 17 red and the 2 fur body circles (page 16). Pin
a slip of paper, with diameter size marked on it, to each red circle as
it is cut and sewn so that it is easy to thread them together in the
correct order.
REINFORCEMENT CIRCLES   Following page 18, attach them to the
smooth sides of the two fur circles.

HEAD

Trace pattern. Cut two pieces in pink cotton. If cotton is thin cut four
pieces and use double.
    Place together, wrong sides to outside. Use pink thread double and
backstitch together, ¼ in (*6 mm*) from the edge, down each side from A
to B. Still using double thread, gather round foot of neck B–B. Draw
up and finish off thread. Turn down and tack raw edges round A–A
at top of head. Turn to right side. Stuff with foam chips. Ladder stitch
across opening.
    Ladder stitch neck to smooth side of a 4¼ in (*11 cm*) diameter red
body circle. Sew round twice, taking thread through both thicknesses
of the red circle to give solidity. Finish off thread underneath circle,
in the centre of the gathers, taking a few stiches into the base of the
neck.

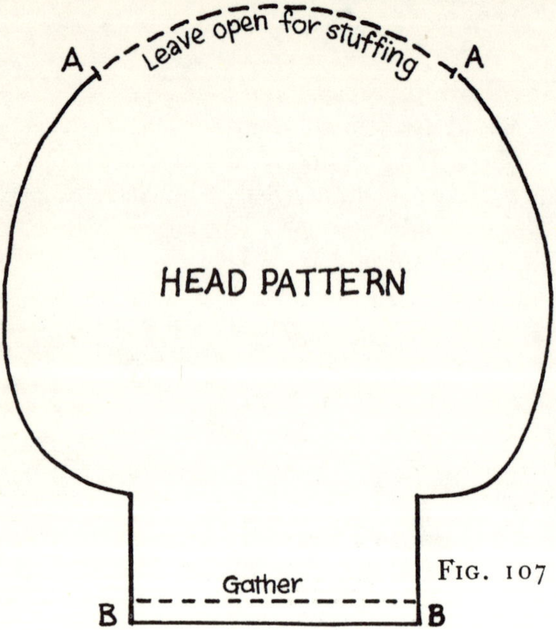

A – – – Leave open for stuffing – – – A

HEAD PATTERN

Gather

B —————————————— B

FIG. 107

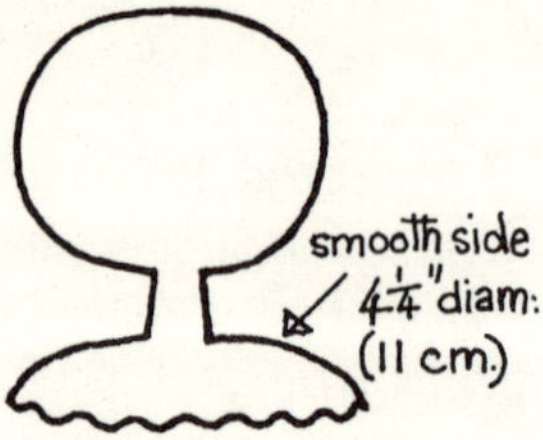

smooth side
4¼" diam.
(11 cm.)

Head sewn to red circle

FIG. 108

HANDS

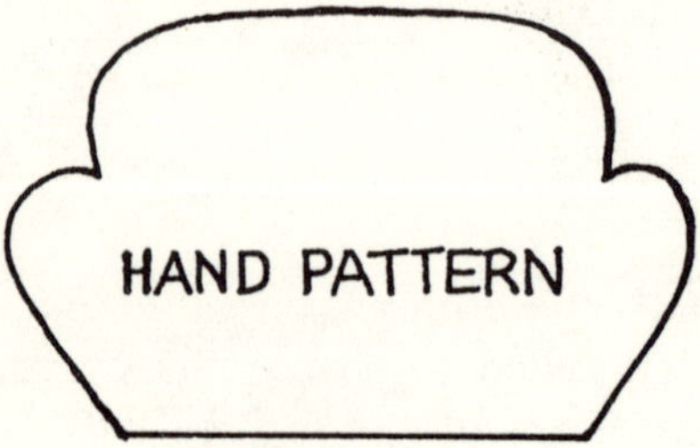

HAND PATTERN

FIG. 109

FIG. 110

Trace pattern.
Cut two in pink
cotton.

On each piece turn up raw edge at
wrist. Use pink thread single to run
gathering thread round wrist. Do not
pull up.

FIG. 111

Fold in half, wrong side to outside. Backstitch (thread single) from A to B, $\frac{1}{4}$ in (*6 mm*) from edge. Turn right side out.

FIG. 112

Stuff with oddment of red fabric. Fold it into oblong shape and push it through wrist. Pull up gathers. Finish off thread by stitching through wrist.

FIG. 113

Fingers: Backstitch three lines with pink thread used single. Sew through all thicknesses.

ARMS

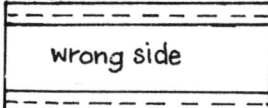

FIG. 114

Turn over long edges of red fabric to wrong side. Tack down.

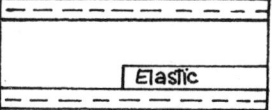

FIG. 115

Place the 6 in (*15 cm*) length of elastic at one end of arm fabric.

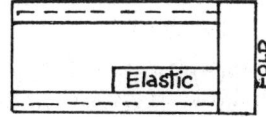

FIG. 116

Fold end over, folding elastic as well. Using red thread double, sew firmly through both thicknesses of material and elastic.

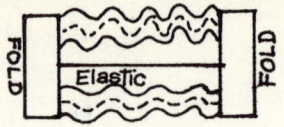

FIG. 117

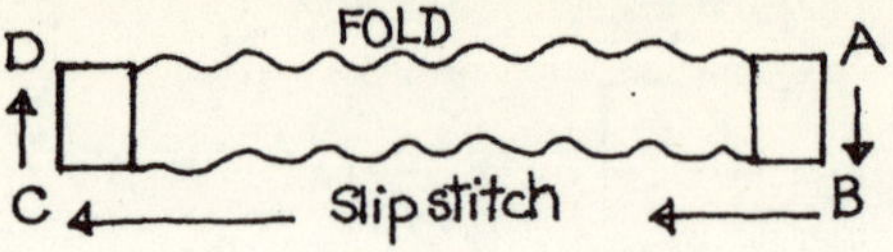

FIG. 118

Repeat at other end of elastic. Do not stretch elastic. Material is deliberately long to allow it to stretch when elastic is pulled. Let material droop in folds.

Fold arm in half lengthwise. Using red thread single, slipstitch edges together: A, B, C, D. Start at A and keep pushing fabric along elastic until seam is stitched. Towards the end it is easier to start a new thread and work from D. Remove tacking threads. Arms should be hanging in loose folds.

FIG. 119

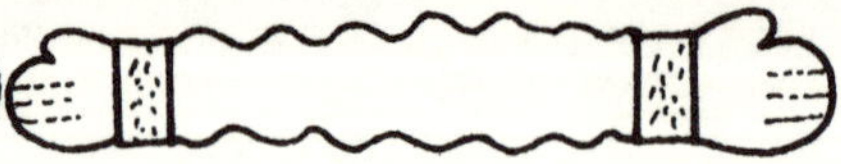

FIG. 120

Ladder stitch hand to each end of arm, using red thread double. Sew round twice. Thumb is on same side as fold.

Fur trimming at wrist. To prevent fraying slipstitch round each piece with white thread used single. Start placing round wrist. Slipstitch one end of hand to arm, then fold fur round wrist overlapping the end. Ladder stitch along overlap, then ladder stitch round the long sides.

HOOD

1. Fold 6½ in × 2½ in (*16·5 cm* × *6·5 cm*) piece of red nylon in half at EA, wrong sides to outside.
2. Backstitch along AB, ¼ in (*6 mm*) from the edge, using thread single.
3. Tack up edge round CBD. Use red thread single and make very small stitches which can be left in.
4. Turn hood to right side.

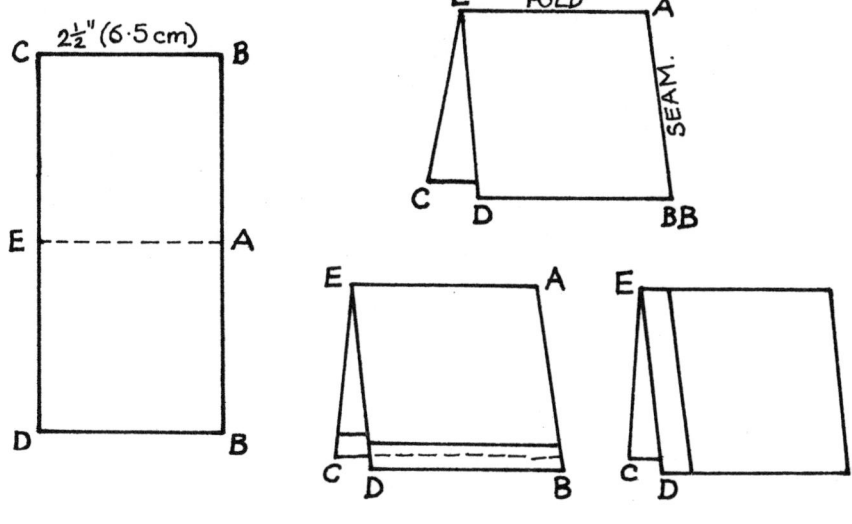

FIG. 121

5. Turn edge CED over on to right side. Pin down. This will be covered with fur trimming.

6. Slipstitch 6 in × ¼ in (*15cm* × *6 mm*) strip of fur all round edge to prevent fraying, with white thread used single.

7. Lay fur strip along edge CED. Use red thread single and oversew on to hood all round.

ASSEMBLY

Attach body elastic to the 4 in (*10 cm*) diameter fur circle which has the reinforcement circle on it (page 19).

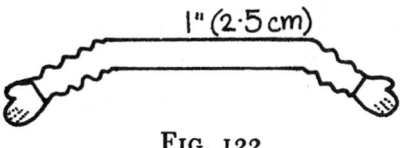

FIG. 122

Find central point of arms. Push folds to each side to leave 1 in (*2·5 cm*) smooth at centre.

65

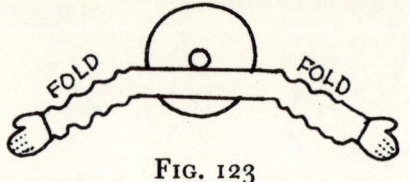

FIG. 123

Stitch this smooth bit of the arms on to gathered side of the fur circle. Folded side of arms is close to central hole through which elastic is emerging. Using red thread double, stitch firmly through red fabric, elastic and all layers of fur on to the reinforcement cotton circle.

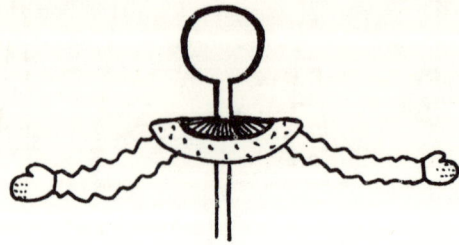

FIG. 124

Place the head and attached red circle on top of the fur circle, to cover reinforcement circle and act as emergency door. Oversew, with red thread used double. Stitch well down into fur base. Now take three or four stitches from red top right through to underside of fur and back again, working round neck and close to it. Pull each stitch tight. When head is pulled to ping the elastic these stitches will keep it firm, as in diagram A, and not let it stretch up as in B.

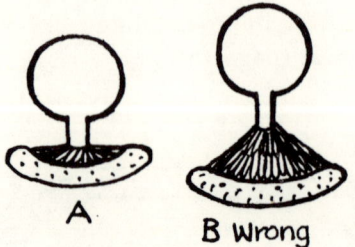

FIG. 125

When emergency door has to be undone these stitches will be apparent and can be snipped.

66

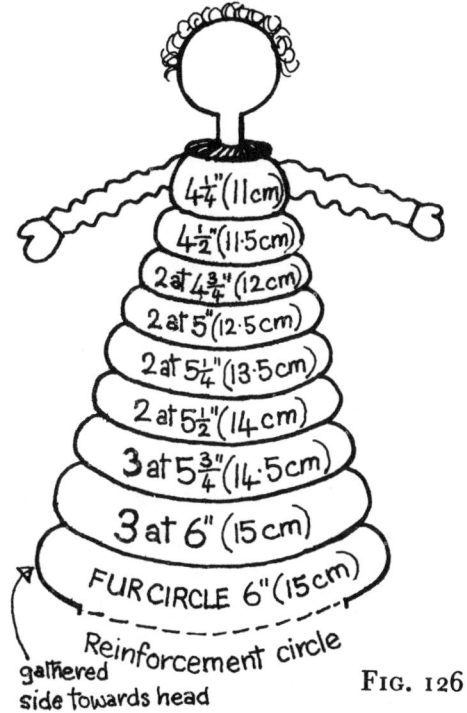

4¼" (11cm)

4½" (11·5cm)

2 at 4¾" (12cm)

2 at 5" (12·5cm)

2 at 5¼" (13·5cm)

2 at 5½" (14cm)

3 at 5¾" (14·5cm)

3 at 6" (15cm)

FUR CIRCLE 6" (15cm)

Reinforcement circle

gathered
side towards head

FIG. 126

Thread up remaining red circles, smooth side towards head, then fur circle as shown. Finish off elastic (page 20).

Emergency Door. Attach 3 in (7·5 cm) diameter red nylon circle to base to cover elastic (page 21). By making it in red it gives the impression of a red cloak trimmed with fur.

FEATURES

Do features before sewing on hood. Thread can be started and finished easily on head knowing it will be covered (Fig. 127).

1. *Eyes.* Stranded cotton (two strands). Satin stitch two circles. Black stranded cotton (single strand). Pupil in centre of eye.

| *Nose and Mouth.* | Red stranded cotton (two strands). | Nose: satin stitch circle.
Mouth: stem stitch. Sew along a few times. |

67

FIG. 127

FIG. 128

2. Animal wool stuck on with Copydex.
Use Copydex carefully: too little and top layer of hair will pull away, too much and a flat pasted look will result.

Eyebrows. Two thin wisps, ½ in (*1·5 cm*) long.
Moustache. One thin wisp, ½ in (*1·5 cm*) long.
Roll wool between fingers to keep hairs close together. Copydex back of hair then press in position. With moustache make sure that nose and mouth are still visible.

Hair. Thicker wisp. 3 in (*7·5 cm*) long. Roll slightly. Copydex back and stick along top seam of head to surround face. Rest remains bald as covered by hood.

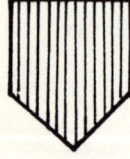

Beard. Cut a 2-in (*5-cm*) length across width of hank of animal wool. Cut edge to shape of beard, as diagram. Copydex top of beard, putting on more than before to soak through slightly to hold beard together. Press hard round face below mouth.

FIG. 129

Hint. When Copydex is dry point of needle can be used to fluff up eyebrows and moustache if they are too flat looking.

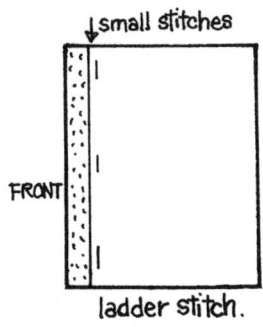

small stitches

FRONT

ladder stitch.

FIG. 130

Hood. Pin hood in position, showing line of hair at front. At back it can either be close to neck or nearer fur trimming, depending on where it fits most neatly.

Use red thread single and ladder stitch back of hood to red circle. A few small stitches can be taken round top of head to hold it to hairline. Take them at back of fur trimming, as shown on diagram, small stitch on the surface, large stitch underneath, and they will be practically invisible.

Hood has to be undone before emergency door can be reached.

Topsyturvy Bridesmaid—Gypsy

FIG. 131

Topsyturvy dolls are an ancient idea. Hold one doll by the waist and turn her upside down. The skirt falls the other way and a completely different doll appears! Doing this amuses a child, but add the pinging of the circles on elastic and the doll becomes an even more fascinating plaything.

Any characters can be made into topsyturvy dolls, by following the patterns to the waist only, but they must have skirts long enough to cover the doll underneath and wide enough to swing over easily when turned upside down.

BRIDESMAID has a silver lamé bodice, pink skirt with net overlay and pink silk skin.

GYPSY has a white blouse, royal blue sash and cuffs, black felt bolero, brilliant orange skirt and oyster satin skin.

70

8a. TOPSYTURVY BRIDESMAID

	BRIDESMAID	GYPSY
Skirt. Circle diameter 18 in (*45 cm*)	Rose pink cotton	Orange cotton
Circle diameter 17½ in (*44·5 cm*)	White net	
Bodies. Circles diameter 4 in (*10 cm*)	9 silver lamé	8 white cotton 1 royal blue cotton
Arms. Circles diameter 2 in (*5 cm*)	30 pink silk	26 white cotton 4 royal blue cotton
Arm Junctions. Square 1½ in (*4 cm*)	White cotton	White cotton
Emergency Doors. Circles diameter 1 in (*2·5 cm*)	2 pink silk	2 royal blue cotton
Necks. Circles diameter 2 in (*5 cm*)	3 pink silk	3 oyster satin
Hands. 2 pieces, each 2¼ in × 1¾ in (*6 cm × 4·5 cm*)	Pink silk	Oyster satin
Heads. 4 pieces, each 3¼ in × 1¾ in (*8·5 cm × 4·5 cm*)	Pink silk	Oyster satin
Backing for Heads (same as heads)	White or pink cotton	White or pink cotton
Reinforcement Circles. 3 circles, diameter 1 in (*2·5 cm*)	Firm cotton, any colour	Firm cotton, any colour
Hair	Thin yellow wool; 2 or 3 shades can be used	Black wool, double knitting: 20 strands, 6 in (*15 cm*) each
Thread. Machine twist	Pink, white	Orange, white, blue, oyster, black
Stranded cotton	Red, black, blue	Red, black brown

72

Filling.   Plastic foam chips.

Thin plastic foam sheeting or tweed:

Hands.   4 pieces, each ¾ in × ½ in (*2 cm* × *1·5 cm*) (2 for Bridesmaid, 2 for Gypsy).

Elastic.   Body: 11 in (*28 cm*) (1 piece only).

Arms: 2 pieces, each 13½ in (*34·5 cm*). Both ³⁄₁₆ in (*5 mm*) wide.

Bridesmaid:

Head-dress. Silver lamé: 1 circle, diameter 1 in (*2·5 cm*). Rose pink cotton: 1 circle, diameter 1 in (*2·5 cm*) cut with pinking shears. Net: 1 circle, diameter 1½ in (*4 cm*).

Bouquet. Silver lamé: 3 circles, diameter 1 in (*2·5 cm*) and 1 circle, diameter 2 in (*5 cm*). Rose pink cotton: 3 circles, diameter 1 in (*2·5 cm*), cut with pinking shears. White pipe-cleaner: 2½ in (*6·5 cm*).

Gypsy:

Tissue Paper. For assembling hair: 2 pieces, each 2 in (*5 cm*) square.

Flower for Hair. Orange cotton: 1 piece 4 in × ½ in (*10 cm* × *1·5 cm*), preferably with selvedge on one long side. Cut other side with pinking shears.

Bolero. Black felt: 1 piece, 4½ in × 3 in. (*11·5 cm* × *7·5 cm*). Gold cord: 1 piece, 18 in (*4·5 cm*) and 1 piece 10 in (*25·5 cm*). Thread to match cord.

If buying material. All 36 in (*90 cm*) wide:

Pink cotton, white net, orange cotton: ½ yard (*45 cm*) will make 2 skirts. White cotton: ¼ yard (*23 cm*). Pink silk: 6 in (*15 cm*). Silver lamé: 4 in (*10 cm*). Oyster satin: 2 in (*5 cm*).

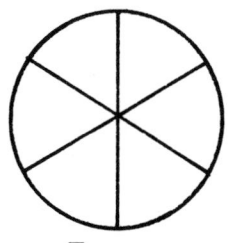

Skirts. Pieces required are rather large. Skirt can be cut in 2, 4 or 6 sections seamed together to make the full size. Allow turnings where pattern is cut. Gypsy's skirt can also be made with each section in a different colour to give a harlequin effect.

Fig. 132

CIRCLES   Gather the circles for bodies, arms and necks (page 16).

73

REINFORCEMENT CIRCLES Following page 18, attach to the smooth sides of 1 pink neck circle, 2 pink arm circles, 1 oyster neck circle and 2 blue arm circles.

HEADS AND HANDS For patterns see Footballer (Figs. 182 and 183, page 94). For instructions for heads see Clown (page 85). For instructions for hands see Wee Willie Winkie (page 53). Use pink thread for Bridesmaid, oyster thread for Gypsy.

SKIRTS

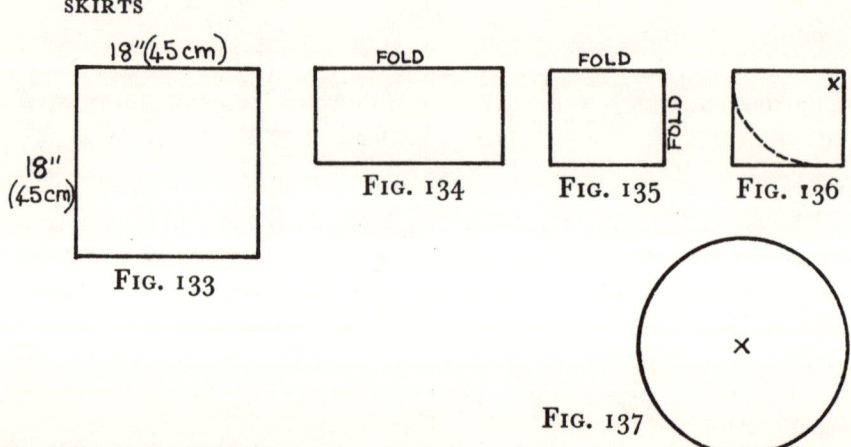

FIG. 133

FIG. 134

FIG. 135

FIG. 136

FIG. 137

To make 18 in (*45 cm*) diameter circle.

1. Cut 18 in (*45 cm*) square of paper. 2. Fold in half. 3. Fold in half again. 4. Make dots 9 in (*23 cm*) from point X (Fig. 136). Cut dotted line. 5. open out.

Cut circles in material. Place pink and orange circles together, wrong sides to outside. Sew ¼ in (*6 mm*) from edge, leaving about 4 in (*10 cm*) open. Sewing can be machining, backstitch or, for speed, running stitch with a backstitch every 2 in (*5 cm*). Turn down raw edges round opening and tack down. Turn inside out. Oversew open edges together with small stitches. Remove tacking thread. Press to get neat edging.

Push hole in centre for elastic, as for gathered circles.

ASSEMBLY

Prepare the two arm elastics (page 22). Sew one to bridesmaid's silver

74

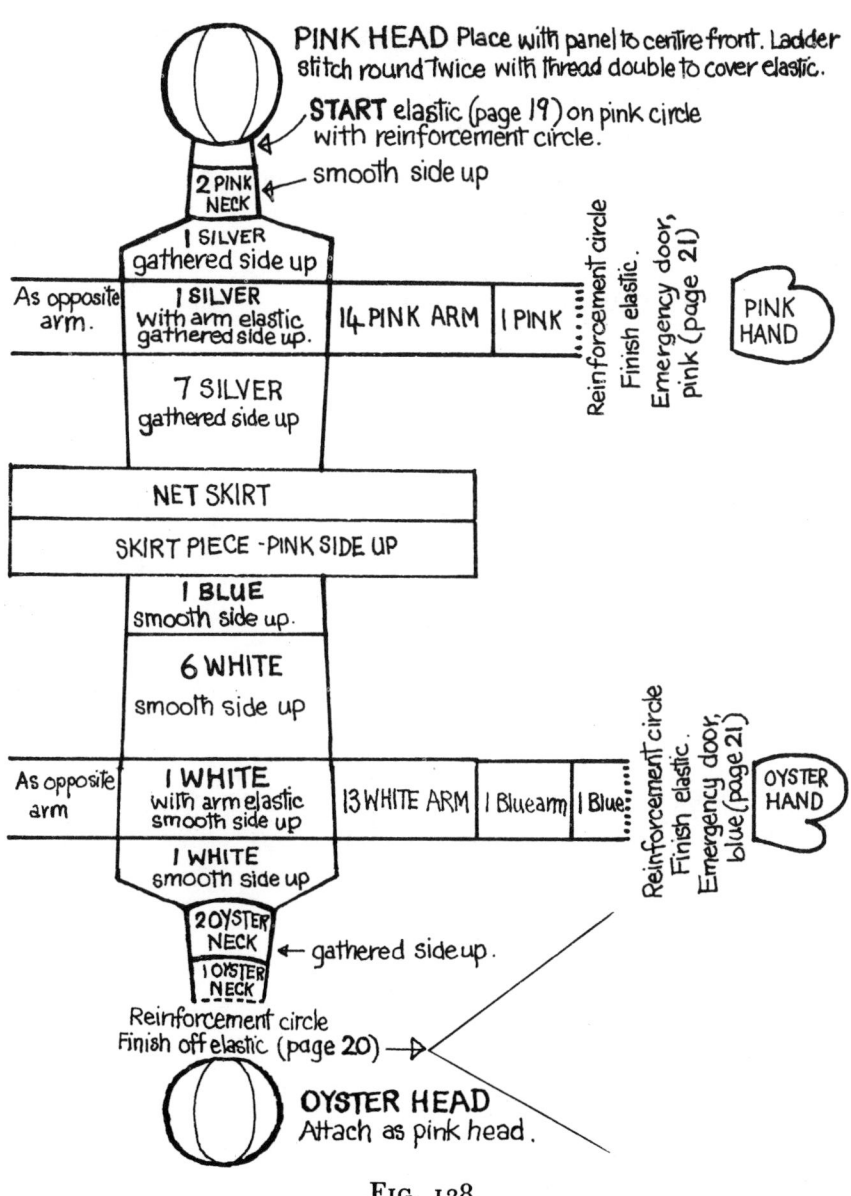

PINK HEAD Place with panel to centre front. Ladder stitch round twice with thread double to cover elastic.

START elastic (page 19) on pink circle with reinforcement circle.

← smooth side up

2 PINK NECK

1 SILVER gathered side up

As opposite arm.

1 SILVER with arm elastic gathered side up.

14 PINK ARM

1 PINK

Reinforcement circle. Finish elastic.

Emergency door, pink (page 21)

PINK HAND

7 SILVER gathered side up

NET SKIRT

SKIRT PIECE - PINK SIDE UP

1 BLUE smooth side up.

6 WHITE smooth side up

As opposite arm

1 WHITE with arm elastic smooth side up

13 WHITE ARM

1 Bluearm

1 Blue

Reinforcement circle. Finish elastic.

Emergency door, blue (page 21)

OYSTER HAND

1 WHITE smooth side up

2 OYSTER NECK

1 OYSTER NECK

← gathered side up.

Reinforcement circle Finish off elastic (page 20) →

OYSTER HEAD Attach as pink head.

FIG. 138

body circle and the other to gypsy's white body circle, both on gathered sides.

Thread rest of circles as Fig. 138. Do arms after bodies and heads are finished. All arm circles gathered side towards body.

Check carefully that elastic is sufficiently taut as skirt makes it easy for circles near waist on other side to slide loose.

FINISHING TOUCHES—BRIDESMAID

Hair

Use thin yellow wool double and twist it round a pencil to make tossing curls all over the head.

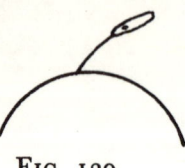

FIG. 139

1. Take a stitch on head to start wool.

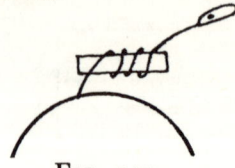

FIG. 140

2. Hold pencil close to head. Wind wool six times round it.

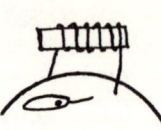

FIG. 141

3. Take another stitch to secure wool.

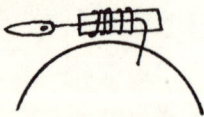

FIG. 142

4. Slip needle through the loops on the pencil.

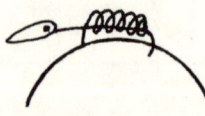

FIG. 143

5. Remove pencil. Take a stitch to fasten curls to head.

FIG. 144

This bunch of loops falls like a ringlet of curls. Bring the needle through to the place where the next curl is required. Carry on like this till the whole head is covered.

Make the loops fairly close together and do them in different directions to make them look natural.

This hair does take quite a lot of wool. If there is any danger of the wool running out do not carry on and finish one colour, then start another, thus making obvious patches. As the wool is used double take one strand of each wool so that the two colours mingle. This gives an even more natural effect than hair all exactly the same shade. Three, or even four, shades of wool can be used if they are mingled in this way.

FIG. 145

Eyes. Stranded cotton (two strands). Satin stitch. Bridesmaid: blue. Gypsy: brown. Black pupil in centre: Two strands. Few satin stitches.
Eyebrows. Black stranded cotton. Stem stitch. Bridesmaid: One strand, one row of stitching. Gypsy: Two strands. Make fairly thick.

Mouth. Red stranded cotton. Stem stitch.
Bridesmaid: Two strands. Thin line.

Gypsy: Four strands. Work along two or three times and make mouth a little longer than bridesmaid.

Nose. Red stranded cotton. Two small straight stitches for nostrils.

Back view
FIG. 146

FIG. 147

FIG. 148

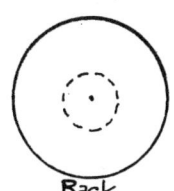

Back.
FIG. 149

Flowers
1. Gather the four 1 in (*2·5 cm*) diameter silver lamé circles. Use thread double. Pull up tight to make silver centres for flowers (Fig. 146). Finish off thread but leave it hanging.
2. Cut the four pink circles nearly into centre to make petals (Fig. 147).
Head-dress
3. Using thread that is hanging from one silver circle, thread on pink petals then net circle (Fig. 148).
4. Still using same thread make circle of gathers at back (Fig. 149). Pull up and front will bunch prettily. Finish off thread.
Toy for Small Child. Place head-dress on centre top of head and take a few stitches through hair.
Toy for Older Child. Put head-dress on head with one pin. The child can

have the fun of changing its position. A number of head-dresses can be made in similar ways, using more layers of net, different shapes, or artificial flowers surrounded by net or silver lamé and child can change them for different weddings.

Bouquet

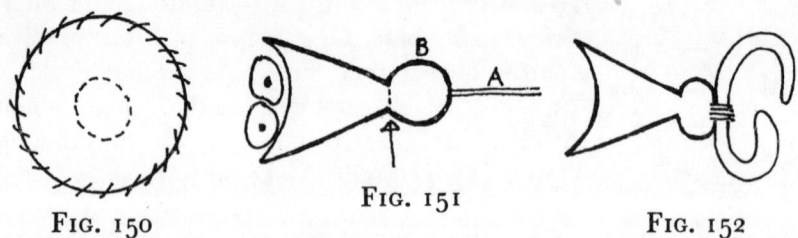

FIG. 150   FIG. 151   FIG. 152

5. Slipstitch round the edge of the 2 in (*5 cm*) diameter silver lamé circle, with thread used single, to prevent fraying. Use thread double to make row of gathers, $\frac{1}{2}$ in (*1·5 cm*) from outer edge (Fig. 150). Do not pull up. Leave thread hanging on wrong side.

6. Make three flowers as paragraphs 1 and 2. Put threads hanging from them through centre of silver circle (take all six threads at once in large-eyed needle). Take a few stitches at centre back to fix it, but leave thread uncut (A on Fig. 151). Pull up gathering thread on silver (see arrow) so that it pulls the silver round the flowers, leaving a handle at the back (B on Fig. 151). Finish off gathering thread.

7. Turn over ends of pipe-cleaner to lose sharp points. Tie the six threads from back of bouquet (A on Fig. 151) round middle of pipe-cleaner. Take three threads each side and knot them. Pipe-cleaner can be bent round doll's wrist to make her hold her bouquet.

Hiding Arm Junction. If desired, use white thread single to ladder stitch once along edges of two silver body circles to join them and conceal junction. Sewing need only go round half the circle.

Not really necessary on gypsy where all is in white.

FINISHING TOUCHES—GYPSY

Hair

Unravel the strands of wool to make them single ply. This gives hair with a bedraggled curly look.

8b. TOPSYTURVEY GYPSY

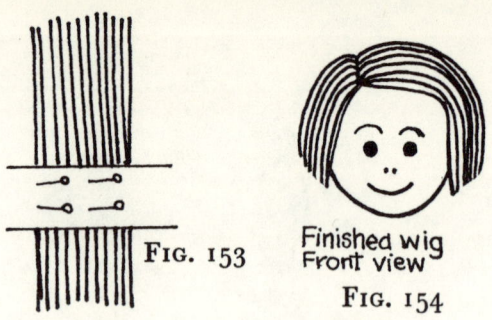

FIG. 153

Finished wig
Front view

FIG. 154

Make a hairpiece as Clown (page 89). Tissue paper is used single as hair is thinner. Make a side parting instead of a centre parting by laying the tissue paper more to one end than to the middle (Fig. 153).
Features. Given under Bridesmaid.

Flower for Hair

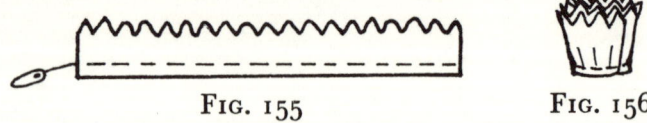

FIG. 155
FIG. 156

If no selvedge available, slipstitch straight edge to prevent fraying. 1. Using orange thread single, gather along selvedge. 2. Pull up tight, letting ends overlap to form a frilly circle (Fig. 156). Finish off thread at back of flower and stitch through hair and head at one side.

Now arrange rest of hair neatly. Use black thread to catch sides of wig together at centre back and take odd stitches to pull hair over any bald patch. Trim ends a little where very long, but keep it raggedly uneven.

Bolero

Trace pattern. Cut one in black felt. Fold it at shoulders to match letters. Oversew A to B, and C to D to make side seams. Turn to right side.

Decoration. Gold cord is ideal. It is held down with matching thread. Lay cord on felt. Take stitches over it at intervals to hold it down.

Design. Shown on bolero pattern used 18 in (*45 cm*) of cord for front. Starting with middle of cord at centre back of neck, each side works to side seam. The 10 in (*25·5 cm*) length starts at centre back of waist and each side works to side seam. Notice that cord is not joined: ends are

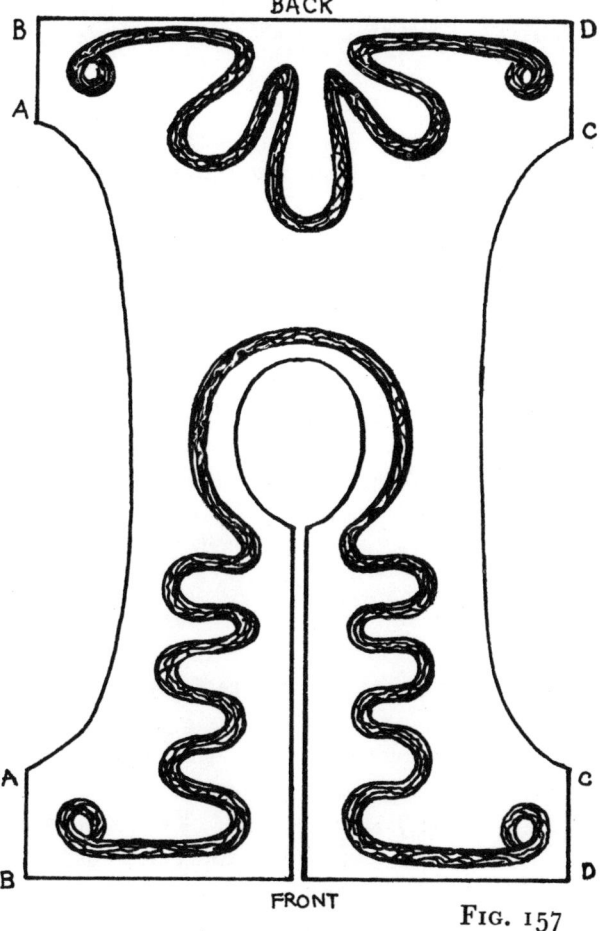

FIG. 157

coiled round ornamentally. Make your own design to use whatever lengths of cord are available.

Alternative. Just put a straight cord round the edges without scrolls. Or leave bolero unadorned.

The cord for the doll in the photograph was tied round packets of envelopes in a gift box of stationery. Use any bright knitting silk, wool with lurez thread in it, narrow ribbon or anything that looks rich and fancy, or use stranded cotton, full thickness, and do stem stitch to make a design.

Tumbler the Clown

Made of a gay assortment of colours and patterns. No two circles need be alike. Ruffles of red satin. Face of white cotton.

MATERIALS

Assorted colours	*Body, legs and arms.*	80 circles, diameter 4 in (*10 cm*).
Red satin	*Ruffles.*	6 circles, diameter 6 in (*15 cm*).
	Nose.	1 circle, diameter 2 in (*5 cm*).
	Mouth.	2 pieces, each 2 in × 1 in (*5 cm × 2·5 cm*).
White cotton	*Head.*	4 pieces, each 5¼ in × 2½ in (*13·5 cm × 6·5 cm*).
	Hands.	2 pieces, each 3¾ in × 2¾ in (*9·5 cm × 7 cm*).
Black cotton	*Feet.*	4 pieces, each 4½ in × 2 in (*11·5 cm × 5 cm*).
Firm cotton, any colour	*Reinforcement Circles.*	5 circles, diameter 1½ in (*4 cm*).
	Arm Junction.	1 piece, 1½ in (*4 cm*) square. Preferably use same cotton as one of the body circles.
Wool	*Hair.*	Brown rug wool, or very thick wool: 30 pieces, each 6 in (*15 cm*).

Thread. Machine twist: Red, white, brown, black and any colour for circles.

Tissue Paper. For assembling hair: 4 pieces, each 2½ in × 1 in (*6·5 cm × 2·5 cm*).

Filling. Plastic foam chips.
Thin plastic foam sheeting or tweed:
    Hands. 2 pieces, each 2 in × 1 in (*5 cm × 2·5 cm*).
    Mouth. 1 piece, 1½ in × ½ in (*4 cm × 1·5 cm*).

9. TUMBLER THE CLOWN

Tweed: *Feet.* 4 pieces, each 4 in × 1¼ in (*10 cm × 3 cm*).
Elastic. Body and Legs: 1 piece, 24 in (*60 cm*). Arms: 1 piece, 14 in (*35·5 cm*). Both ¼ in (*6 mm*) wide.
If buying material. To make body, legs and arms all in one colour: 1 yard (*90 cm*) of 36-in (*90-cm*) wide material.
Ruffles: 6 in (*15 cm*) of 36-in (*90-cm*) wide material.

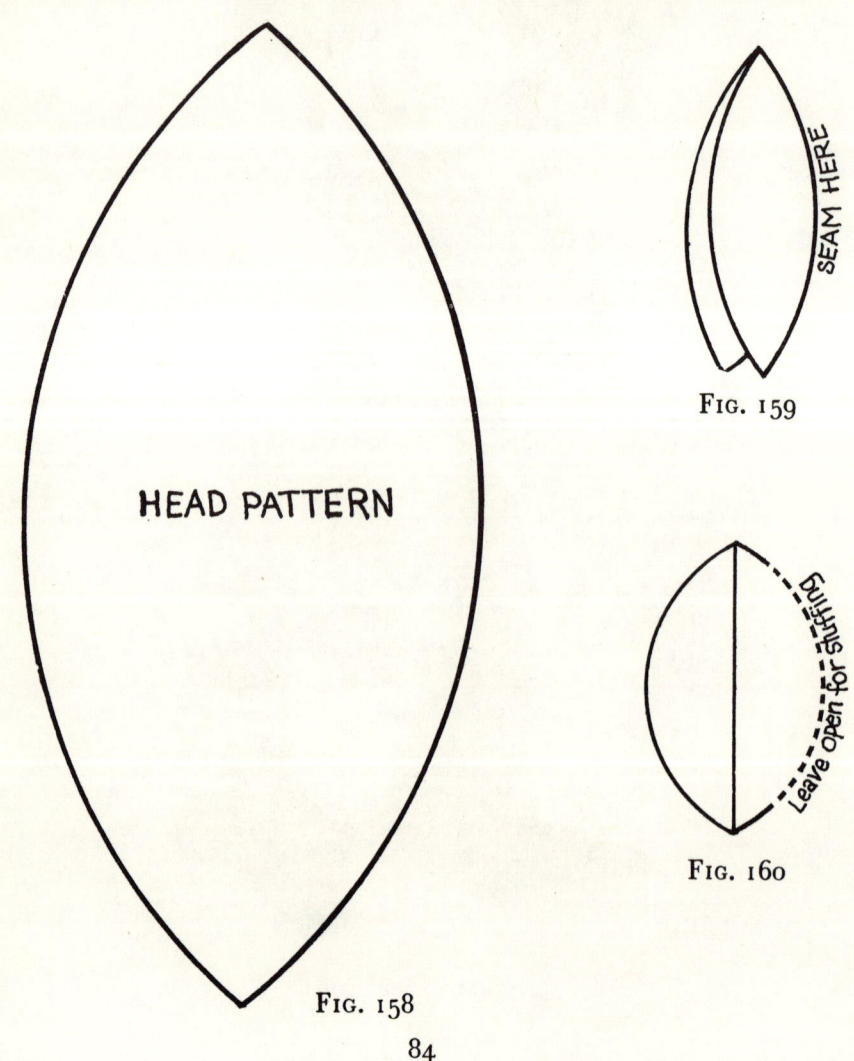

HEAD PATTERN

SEAM HERE

FIG. 159

Leave open for stuffing

FIG. 160

FIG. 158

CIRCLES   Gather the 80 assorted coloured circles and the 6 red satin circles for ruffles (page 16).

REINFORCEMENT CIRCLES   Following page 18, attach one circle to the gathered side of a red satin ruffle circle, two to the smooth sides of two red satin ruffle circles and two to the smooth sides of two of the 4 in (*10 cm*) diameter circles.

HEAD

1. Trace pattern. Cut four pieces in white cotton.
2. Place two pieces together, wrong sides to outside. Backstitch along one side (Fig. 159) $\frac{1}{4}$ in (*6 mm*) from edge. Use thread double.
3. Repeat with the other two pieces.
4. Lay these two sections together. Backstitch round edge, leaving opening as shown dotted (Fig. 160).
5. Turn back raw edges round opening. Tack down.
6. Turn to right side. Stuff with plastic foam chips. Ladder stitch along hole to close it, using thread double.

HANDS

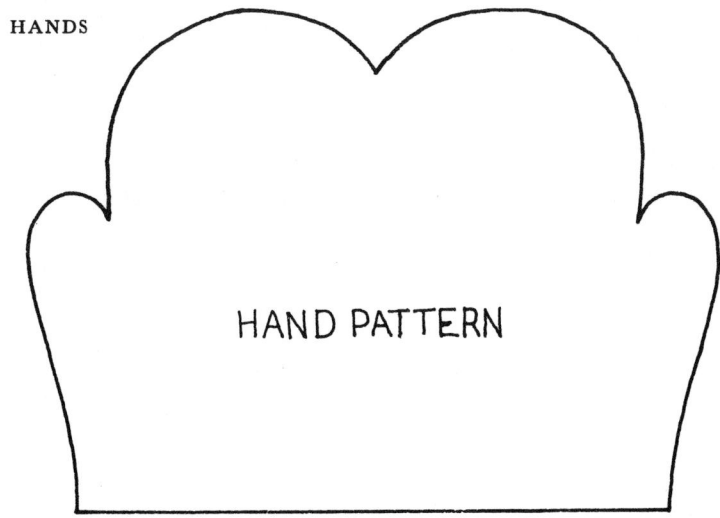

HAND PATTERN

FIG. 161

Trace pattern. Cut two in white cotton.

FIG. 162

FIG. 163

On each piece turn up raw edge at wrist.

Use white thread double to run gathering thread round wrist. Do not pull up.

Fold in half, wrong side to outside. Backstitch (thread single) from A to B ¼ in (*6 mm*) from edge. Turn to right side.

FIG. 164

FIG. 165

Slip a 2 in (*5 cm*) × 1 in (*2·5 cm*) piece of foam sheeting or tweed inside hand.
Fingers: Backstitch three lines with white thread used double. Sew through all thicknesses.

Slip a few foam chips inside palm of hand to make it puffy. Pull up gathers. Finish off thread by stitching through wrist.

FEET

Trace pattern. Outer line is shoe. Cut four pieces in black cotton. Shaded part is shoe lining. Cut four pieces in tweed.

Lay each piece of tweed on wrong side of a shoe piece (as shown on pattern).

86

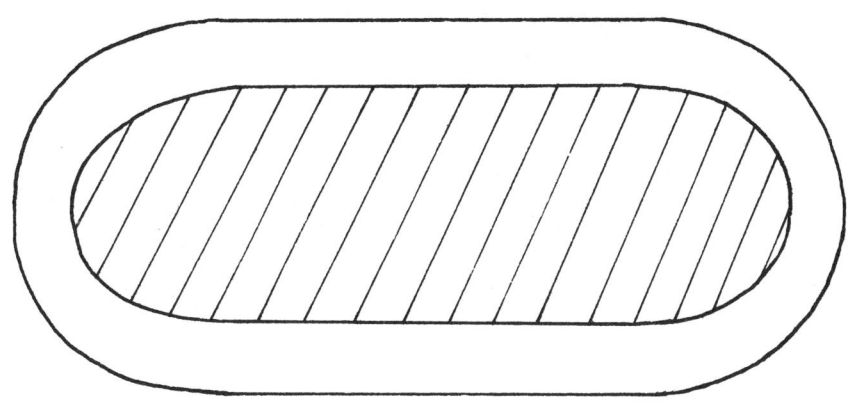

FOOT PATTERN

FIG. 166

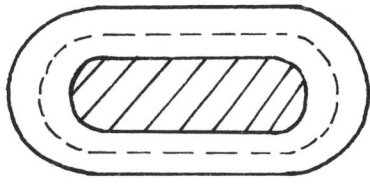

FIG. 167

Turn edge of shoe on to lining.
Tack down. If stitches are taken
only on to tweed they will not
show on right side and can be left
in.

FIG. 168

Pin two finished pieces on top of
each other, right sides to outside.
Blanket stitch together round
edge, using red thread double.

ASSEMBLY

Prepare arm elastic and sew to smooth side of the body circle that
matches the arm junction (page 22).

For rest of assembly follow basic method on page 23, in that order.
All circles gathered side towards head, unless otherwise stated.

Feet. Ladder stitch a shoe to red ruffle at end of each leg. Using red
thread double, sew round twice. Sew round back of heel and across

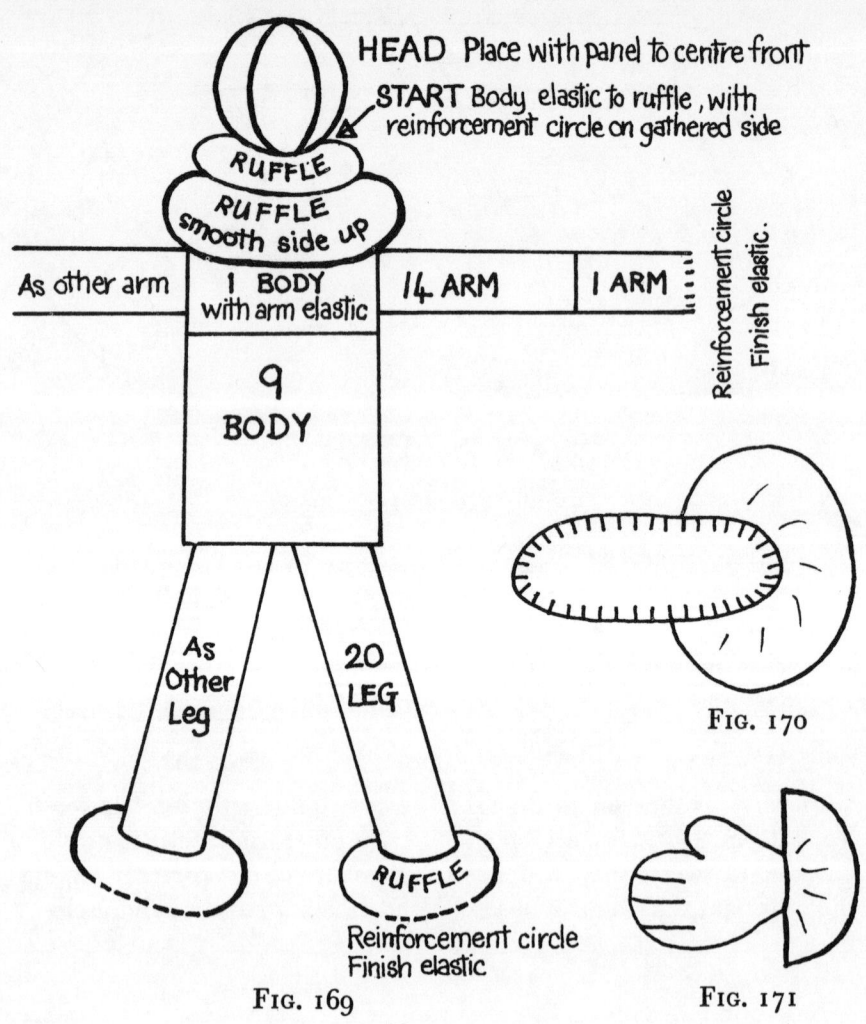

HEAD Place with panel to centre front

START Body elastic to ruffle, with reinforcement circle on gathered side

RUFFLE

RUFFLE smooth side up

| As other arm | 1 BODY
with arm elastic | 14 ARM | 1 ARM | Reinforcement circle
Finish elastic. |

9 BODY

As Other Leg

20 LEG

RUFFLE

Reinforcement circle
Finish elastic

FIG. 169

FIG. 170

FIG. 171

front of foot. This covers reinforcement circle and acts as emergency door.

Hands. Sew wrist to centre of red satin ruffle circle. Sew to gathered side, taking a few stitches through centre of circle. Then ladder stitch round wrist on to gathers.

Ladder stitch this ruffle to the end of the arm, it covers reinforcement circle and acts as emergency door. Sew round edge of reinforcement circle which leaves outer edges of both ruffle and arm circle free.

Hair

Lay two pieces of tissue paper on flat surface.

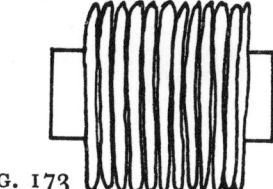

FIG. 172

Lay the strands of rug wool across paper.

FIG. 173

Lay the other two pieces of tissue paper on top. Pin together.

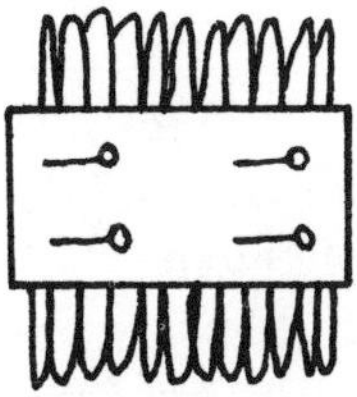

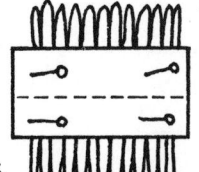

FIG. 174

Using brown thread double, backstitch along centre, through paper and wool. Tear away paper on under side.

FIG. 175

Pin wig on top of head. The stitching forms centre parting. Arrange hair so that head seams will come to each side of face as shown. Backstitch again along parting, going through head as well.

FIG. 176

Tear away top paper to leave a mop of hair.

FIG. 177

89

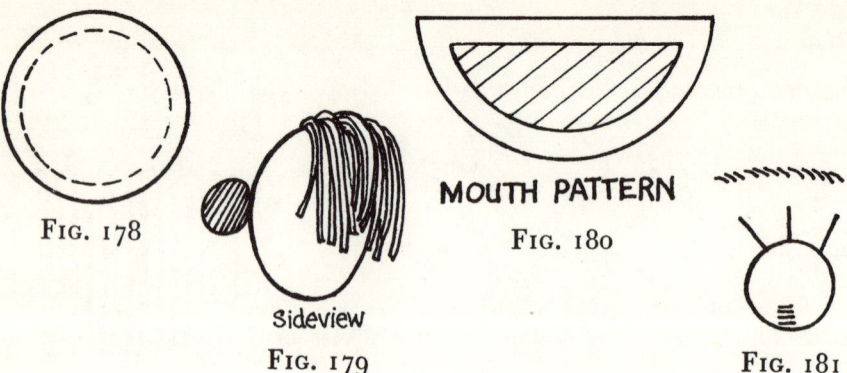

FIG. 178

Sideview
FIG. 179

MOUTH PATTERN
FIG. 180

FIG. 181

Nose

1. Red satin circle, diameter 1 in (*2·5 cm*). Using thread double, gather round edge (Fig. 178). Pull half up. Stuff with foam chips or tiny bits of tweed. Pull up tightly.

2. Finish off and ladder stitch to centre of face, using same thread. Sew round twice.

Mouth

3. Trace pattern. Mouth: Cut to outer edge. Cut two in red satin. Mouth padding: Cut to shaded part. Cut one in foam sheeting or tweed.

Place satin bits together, wrong sides to outside. Backstitch round curve, using thread double. Turn over edges of straight side. Tack down. Turn right side out. Slip in foam. Slipstitch across opening. Use red thread double to ladder stitch to face. Sew round twice.

Eye

4. Embroider eyes with black thread used double. Use satin stitch for centre, backstitch round outer edge, straight stitches for eyelashes, and stem stitch (working along two or three times) for eyebrows (Fig. 181).

Footballer

Blue and white striped shirt, blue pants, blue and white striped socks, black boots and flesh-coloured head, hands and knees.

Make him in your local football club's colours.

THIS PATTERN CAN BE USED FOR AN ORDINARY BOY

Use the circles for the legs of pants down to feet to make him wear long trousers.

Change colours and add cloak, hat or other details to make any male character in history or fiction.

MATERIALS

Royal blue cotton	*Body.*	8 circles, diameter 4 in (*10 cm*) (4 for shirt, 4 for pants).
	Legs of Pants.	14 circles, diameter 3 in (*7·5 cm*) (7 for each leg.)
	Arms and Socks.	24 circles, diameter 2 in (*5 cm*) (8 for each arm, 4 for each sock).
	Emergency Doors.	For wrists: 2 circles, diameter 1 in (*2·5 cm*).
White cotton	*Body.*	4 circles, diameter 4 in (*10 cm*) (for shirt).
	Arms and Socks.	20 circles, diameter 2 in (*5 cm*) (7 for each arm, 3 for each sock).
	Arm Junction.	1 piece, 1½ in (*4 cm*) square. 1 circle, diameter 1½ in (*4 cm*).
Fiesh-coloured cotton	*Head.*	4 pieces, each 3¼ in × 1¾ in (*8·5 cm × 4·5 cm*). Use double if material is flimsy.
	Neck and Knees.	19 circles, diameter 2 in (*5 cm*) (3 for neck, 8 for each knee).

IO. FOOTBALLER

	Hands.	2 pieces, each $2\frac{1}{4}$ in $\times$ $1\frac{3}{4}$ in (*6 cm $\times$ 4·5 cm*).
	Ears.	4 pieces, each $1\frac{1}{4}$ in $\times$ 1 in (*3 cm $\times$ 2·5 cm*).
Black cotton	*Boots.*	4 pieces, each $2\frac{1}{4}$ in $\times$ $1\frac{1}{2}$ in (*6 cm $\times$ 4 cm*).
Firm cotton, any colour	*Reinforcement Circles.*	5 circles, diameter 1 in (*2·5 cm*).
Brown wool	*Hair.*	Small ball, 3 or 4 ply.

Thread. Machine twist: Royal blue, white, flesh and black.
Stranded cotton: Red, blue and black.

Filling. Plastic foam chips.
Thin plastic foam sheeting or tweed: *Hands.* 2 pieces, each $\frac{3}{4}$ in $\times$ $\frac{1}{2}$ in (*2 cm $\times$ 1·5 cm*).
Tweed: *Feet.* 4 pieces, each $1\frac{3}{4}$ in $\times$ $\frac{3}{4}$ in (*4·5 cm $\times$ 2 cm*).

Elastic. Body and legs: 1 piece, 20 in (*51 cm*). Arms: 1 piece, 11 in (*28 cm*). Both $\frac{3}{16}$ in (*5 mm*) wide.

If buying material. Royal blue: 12 in (*30 cm*) of 36-in (*90-cm*) wide material.
White and flesh: $\frac{1}{4}$ yard (*23 cm*) of 36-in (*90-cm*) wide material of each will do two footballers.

CIRCLES Gather the circles for the body, legs of pants, arms (but not arm junction), socks, neck and knees (page 16). Into one white shirt circle slip the circle for arm junction before pulling up gathers.

REINFORCEMENT CIRCLES Following page 18, attach one circle to the smooth side of a neck circle, and the other four to the smooth sides of four blue arm and sock circles.

HEAD

Trace pattern. Cut four pieces in flesh-coloured cotton. Make as Clown's head (page 85). If material is flimsy cut another four pieces and use double, or cut the extra pieces in white or pink cotton.

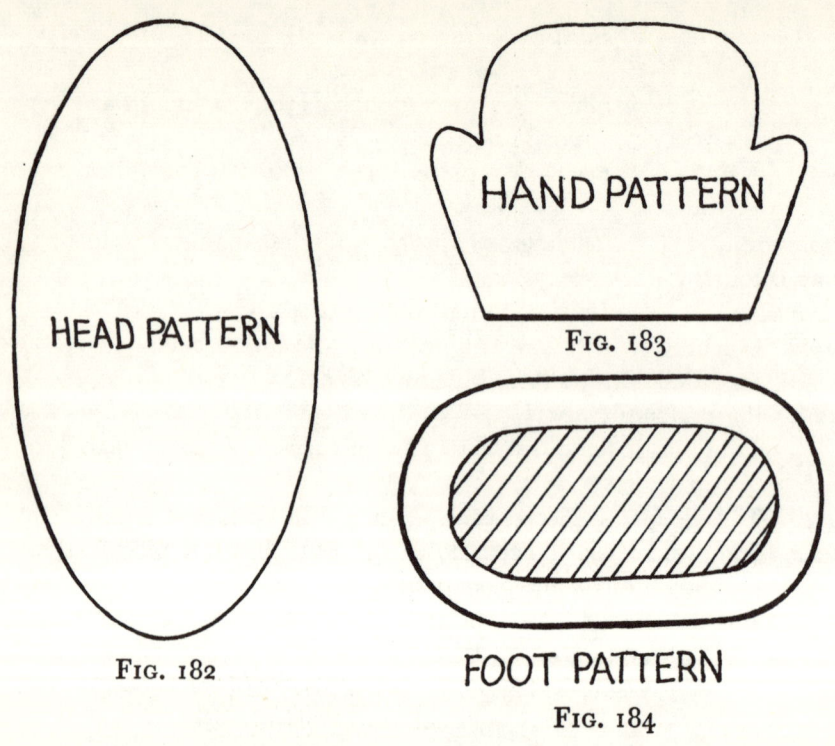

HEAD PATTERN

Fig. 182

HAND PATTERN

Fig. 183

FOOT PATTERN

Fig. 184

HANDS

Trace pattern. For each hand cut two pieces in flesh-coloured cotton. Make as Wee Willie Winkie's hand (page 53).

BOOTS

Trace pattern. Outer line is boot: Cut four pieces in black cotton. Shaded part is boot lining: Cut four pieces in tweed. Make as Clown's foot (page 87). Sew outer edge with black thread.

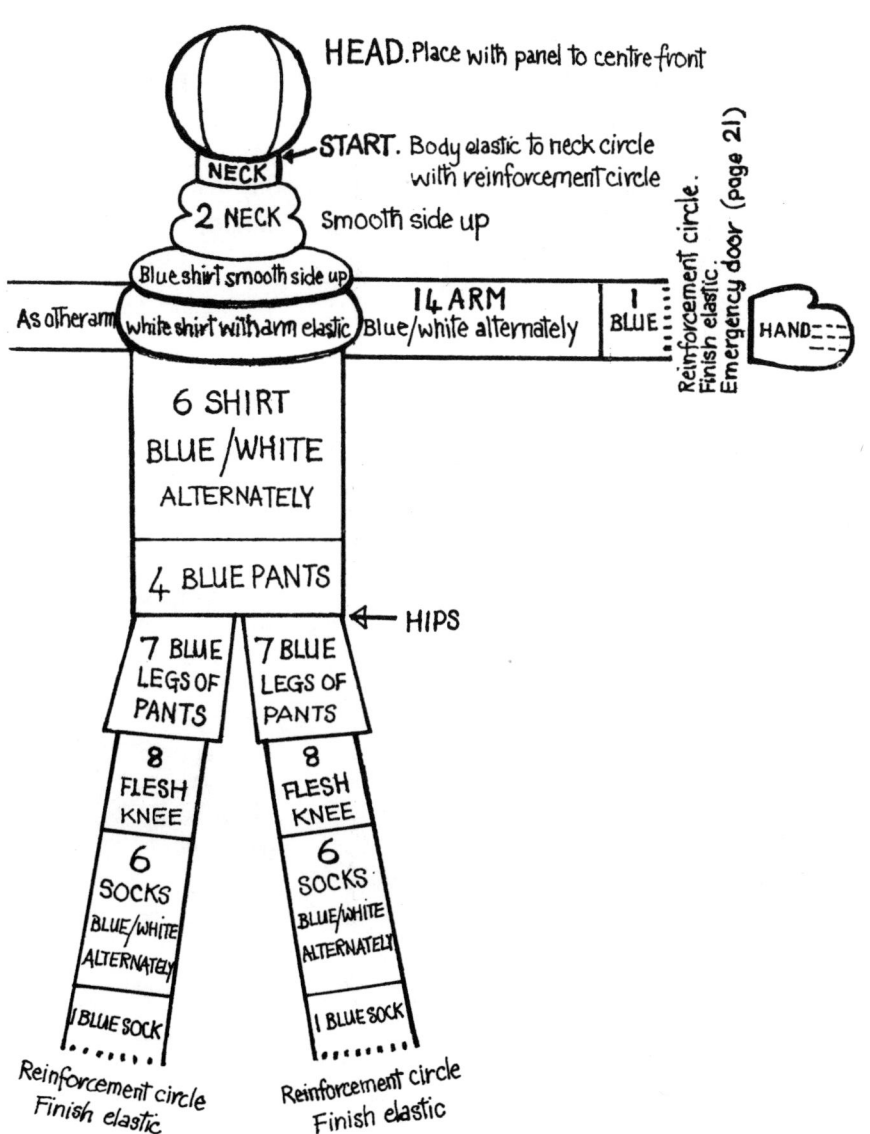

HEAD. Place with panel to centre front

START. Body elastic to neck circle
with reinforcement circle

NECK

2 NECK ⟩ Smooth side up

Blue shirt smooth side up

As other arm | white shirt with arm elastic | 14 ARM Blue/white alternately | 1 BLUE | HAND

Reinforcement circle.
Finish elastic.
Emergency door (page 21)

6 SHIRT
BLUE /WHITE
ALTERNATELY

4 BLUE PANTS

← HIPS

7 BLUE LEGS OF PANTS | 7 BLUE LEGS OF PANTS

8 FLESH KNEE | 8 FLESH KNEE

6 SOCKS BLUE/WHITE ALTERNATELY | 6 SOCKS BLUE/WHITE ALTERNATELY

1 BLUE SOCK | 1 BLUE SOCK

Reinforcement circle
Finish elastic

Reinforcement circle
Finish elastic

FIG. 185

ASSEMBLY

Prepare arm elastic and sew to gathered side of the white shirt circle that has the arm junction circle inside it (page 22).

For rest of assembly follow basic method on page 23, in that order. All circles gathered side towards head unless otherwise stated.

Sew black boot on to each leg to act as emergency door, using thread double. Ladder stitch twice round heel and across front of foot.

EARS

Trace pattern. Cut four pieces in flesh-coloured cotton. Make as Wee Willie Winkie's ear (page 54). Ladder stitch one ear to each side of head about halfway down. It will come into centre of a panel.

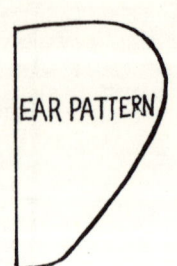

EAR PATTERN

FIG. 186

HAIR

Make as Wee Willie Winkie's hair (page 56).

FEATURES

Eyes. Blue thread, used double: Satin stitch eye. Black thread, used double: Stem stitch eyebrows and take a few stitches in centre of blue eye.

Mouth. Red thread, used double: Stem stitch wide curving mouth working along row about five times.

Nose. Two little straight stitches in red.

FIG. 187

HIDING ARM JUNCTION   If desired, use blue thread single to ladder stitch along edge of two body circles to join them and conceal junction. Sewing need only go round half the circle.

Little Red Riding-Hood

Blue cotton dress and pants, with white apron and socks and red brushed nylon cloak. Flesh or pink cotton for head, hands and legs. Cloak and apron come off.

THIS PATTERN CAN BE USED FOR AN ORDINARY GIRL

Without her cloak and apron she is just wearing a simple dress.

Make all the arm circles in flesh and the dress will be sleeveless.

Add a few inches to the skirt to make a full-length ball gown: make it in silk and give her silver or gold lamé shoes.

MATERIALS

Light blue cotton	*Body.*	12 circles, diameter 4 in (*10 cm*) (8 for bodice, 4 for pants).
	Sleeves and Legs of Pants.	14 circles, diameter 2 in (*5 cm*) (6 for each arm, 1 for each leg).
	Skirt.	1 piece, 12 in × 4 in (*30 cm × 10 cm*).
	Arm Junction.	1 piece, 1½ in (*4 cm*) square. 1 circle, diameter 1½ in (*4 cm*).
Flesh or pink cotton	*Head.*	4 pieces, each 3¼ in × 1¾ in (*8·5 cm × 4·5 cm*). Use double if material is flimsy.
	Neck, Arms and Legs.	49 circles, diameter 2 in (*5 cm*) (3 for neck, 9 for each arm, 14 for each leg).
	Hands.	2 pieces, each 2¼ in × 1¾ in (*6 cm × 4·5 cm*).
	Emergency Doors.	2 circles, diameter 1 in (*2·5 cm*).
White cotton	*Socks.*	14 circles, diameter 2 in (*5 cm*) (7 for each leg.)
	Apron.	1 piece, 3 in × 2½ in (*7·5 cm × 6·5 cm*).
	Apron tie.	1 piece, 25 in × 1 in (*63·5 cm × 2·5 cm*).
Black cotton	*Shoes.*	4 pieces, each 2¼ in × 1½ in (*6 cm × 4 cm*).

11. LITTLE RED RIDING-HOOD

98

Red brushed nylon *Cloak.* 1 piece, 13 in × 10 in (*33 cm* × *25·5 cm*).

Firm cotton, *Reinforcement Circles.* 5 circles, diameter 1 in (*2·5* any colour *cm*).

Yellow wool *Hair.* Small ball, 3 or 4 ply.

Red ribbon *Cloak.* 14 in (*35·5 cm*) narrow ribbon.

White lace *Apron.* 3½ in (*9 cm*) narrow lace.

Tissue paper. For assembling hair: 2 pieces, each 1½ in (*4 cm*) square.

String. Basket: Small ball of fine string.

Crochet Hook. No. 0.

Thread. Machine twist: Light blue, flesh, white, black, red and yellow.

Stranded cotton: Red, black and blue.

Filling. Plastic foam chips.

Thin plastic foam sheeting or tweed:

Hands. 2 pieces, each ¾ in × ½ in (*2 cm* × *1·5 cm*).

Tweed: *Feet.* 4 pieces, each 1¾ in × ¾ in (*4·5 cm* × *2 cm*).

Elastic. Body and legs: 1 piece, 20 in (*51 cm*). Arms: 1 piece, 11 in (*28 cm*). Both ³⁄₁₆ in (*5 mm*) wide.

If buying material. Blue cotton: ¼ yard (*23 cm*) of 36-in (*90-cm*) wide material.

Flesh cotton: ¼ yard (*23 cm*) of 36-in (*90-cm*) wide material.

White cotton: ¼ yard (*23 cm*) of 36-in (*90-cm*) wide material will make three sets of aprons and socks.

CIRCLES Gather circles for the body, sleeves, legs of pants, neck, arms (but not arm junction), legs and socks (page 16). Into one body circle slip the circle for arm junction before pulling up gathers.

REINFORCEMENT CIRCLES Following page 18, attach two circles to the smooth sides of two white sock circles and three circles to the smooth sides of three flesh arm and neck circles.

HEAD, HANDS, SHOES Patterns as Footballer (page 94).

Instructions: Head as Clown (page 85).

Hands as Wee Willie Winkie (page 53).

Shoes as Clown (page 87). Sew outer edge with black thread.

gathers

4"
(10cm)

←side
seam

narrow hem

FIG. 188

Finished skirt

FIG. 189

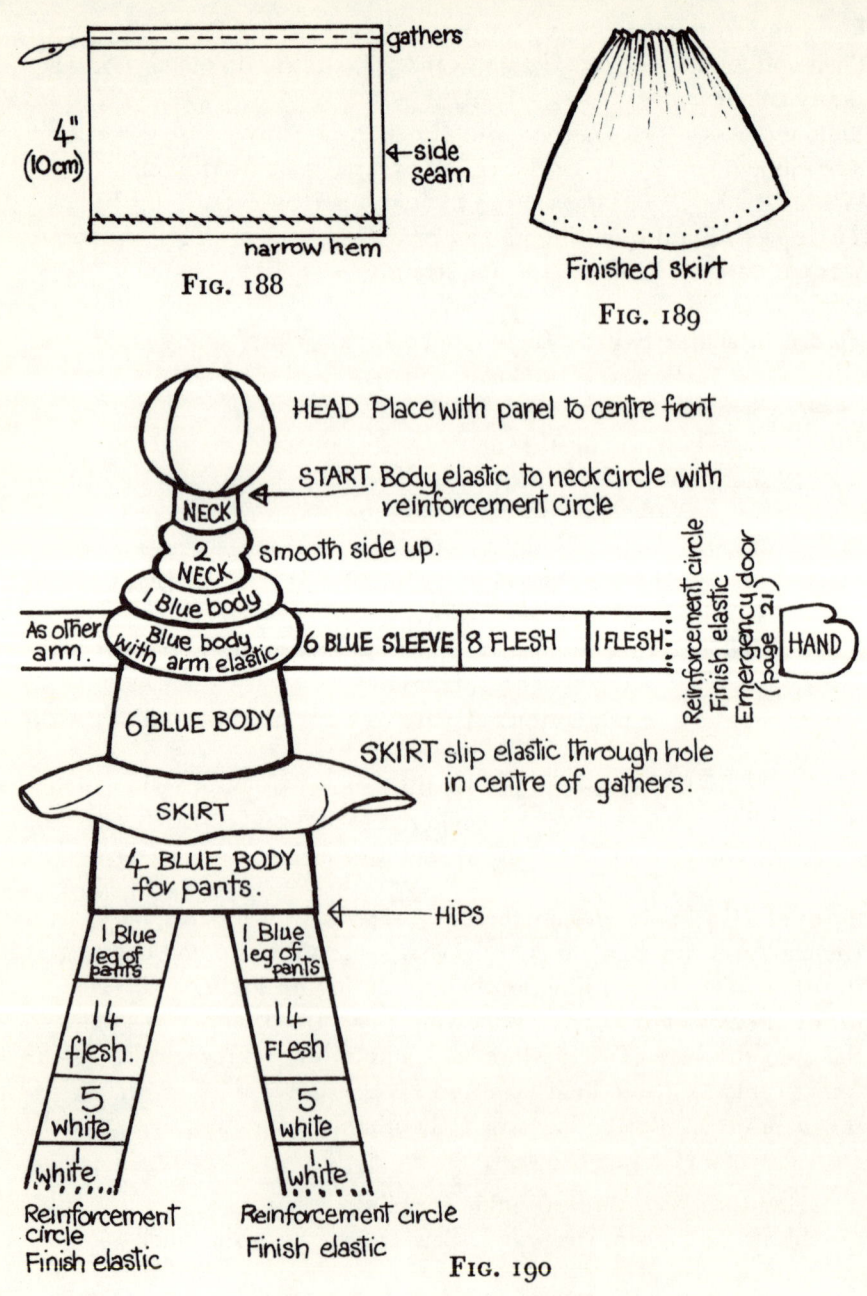

HEAD Place with panel to centre front

START. Body elastic to neck circle with
reinforcement circle

NECK

2
NECK   smooth side up.

1 Blue body

As other
arm.   Blue body   6 BLUE SLEEVE   8 FLESH   I FLESH   HAND
          with arm elastic

6 BLUE BODY

SKIRT slip elastic through hole
in centre of gathers.

SKIRT

4 BLUE BODY
for pants.

HIPS

1 Blue   1 Blue
leg of   leg of
pants   pants

14   14
flesh.   FLESH

5   5
white   white

white   white

Reinforcement   Reinforcement circle
circle   Finish elastic
Finish elastic

Reinforcement circle
Finish elastic
Emergency door
(page 21)

FIG. 190

100

SKIRT

Take strip of blue cotton. Fold in half, so that short ends come together, wrong side to outside. Use thread single to backstitch ¼ in (*6 mm*) from edge, to make side seam of skirt. Press seam flat.

On one long side turn up narrow hem. Hem with small stitches.

On other long side turn over top about ¼ in (*6 mm*). Use thread double and gather as near folded edge as possible. Pull up tightly and finish off thread. Turn to right side.

Hint. If selvedge is available for one long side, material can be gathered along selvedge without turning over edge. Skirt need then only be cut 12 in × 3¾ in (*30 cm × 9·5 cm*).

ASSEMBLY

Prepare arm elastic and sew to gathered side of the blue body circle that has the arm junction circle inside it (page 22).

For rest of assembly follow basic method on page 23, in that order.

All circles gathered side towards head, unless otherwise stated.

Sew black shoe to each leg to act as emergency door, using thread double. Ladder stitch twice round heel and across front of foot.

HAIR   Yellow wool.

Backstitch→

Fringe. Cut 2 in (*5 cm*) lengths. Lay across top of face. Start about ¼ in (*6 mm*) behind centre top point, letting ends fall down over face. They can be trimmed later which is easier than trying to keep them straight at this stage. Using yellow thread single, backstitch along strands stitching well into head. Turn and stitch back.

Fig. 191

Rest of Hair. Cut 6 in (*15 cm*) lengths. Use the tissue paper to make a wig as described in Clown (page 89). Paper can be used single as wool is thin. Put in plenty of wool. When made, sew wig on top of head with front just overlapping fringe. At back of head take a few stitches through wool (x x on lower diagram) to pull sides together and cover back.

Back of head

Trim ends of hair and fringe.

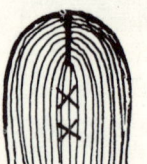

Fig. 192

FEATURES

Eyes. Black stranded cotton (single strand). Outline eye with running stitch to get shape correct. Then go over it with stem stitch. Eyelashes: Four straight stitches. Eyebrows: Stem stitch. Blue stranded cotton (two strands). Satin stitch circle. Black: a few tiny stitches in centre of blue.

Fig. 193

Mouth. Red stranded cotton (four strands). Stem stitch curved smiling mouth, going along about three times.
Nose. Two little straight stitches for nostrils.

APRON

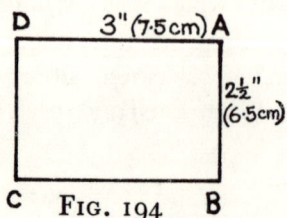

Fig. 194

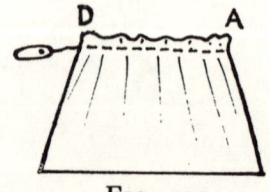

Fig. 195

Turn up and sew narrow hem round AB, BC, CD.

Gather raw edge AD. Pull up slightly. Finish off thread.

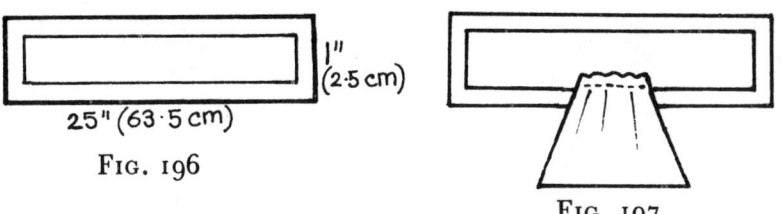

FIG. 196

25" (63·5 cm)   1" (2·5 cm)

FIG. 197

Turn over all edges of apron tie. Tack down.

Lay gathered edge in centre of strip.

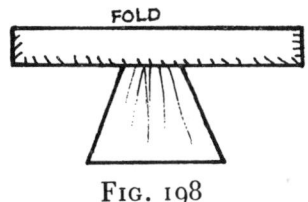

FOLD

FIG. 198

Fold strip in half concealing gathers. Oversew edges, hemming at front and back where strip passes over apron.

Lace Edging. Turn in ends of lace. Hem across foot of apron.

CLOAK

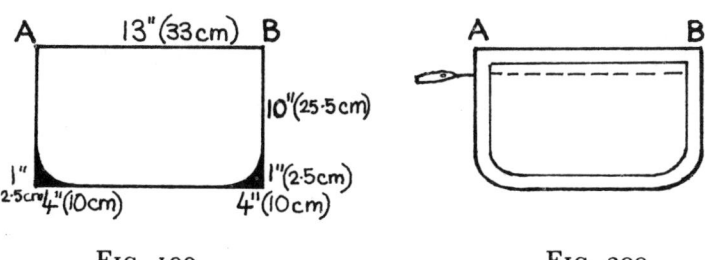

A   13" (33 cm)   B

10" (25·5 cm)

1" 2·5 cm   4" (10 cm)   1" (2·5 cm) 4" (10 cm)

FIG. 199

A   B

FIG. 200

Shape cloak: Measure 4 in (*10 cm*) from bottom corners on long side, 1 in (*2·5 cm*) on short side. Cut curved line between these points as shown shaded.

Turn over edges and stitch narrow hem all round. Gather edge AB. Gather just below hem, using red thread double. Pull up gathers to measure 5½ in (*14 cm*). Finish off thread.

FIG. 201

Hem will make a little frill round face when cloak is worn. (If using different materials try cloak on head. Gather to fit neatly round face but not tightly.)

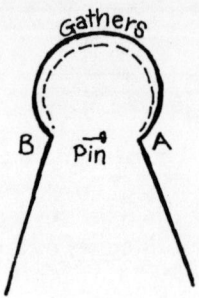

FIG. 202

Pin gathers to head at forehead. At back of head put pin through cloak (not doll) where back of neck comes (see diagram).

Remove cloak. Lay it flat on table, right side with pin upwards.

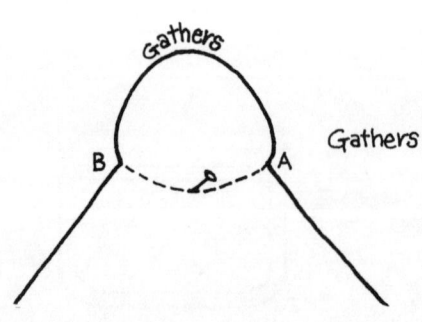

FIG. 202a

Gather, from one end of the gathers, A, in a curved line to the pin, then curving back to other end of gathers, B. Use red thread double. This shape need not be precise so do not hesitate to stitch without marking guide lines.

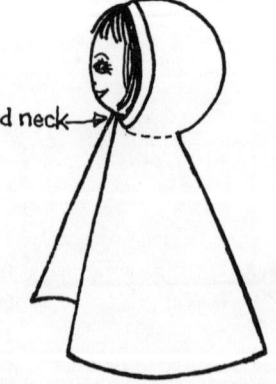

Gathers round neck →

FIG. 202b

Pull up gathers slightly. Try cloak on doll again to make sure it fits round the neck: not a tight fit as there are ribbon ties. Fasten off gathers.

Ribbons. Cut the 14-in (*35·5-cm*) length of red ribbon in half. Fold under one end of each piece. Sew to each side of cloak at chin, where neck gathers meet round face. Tie a bow under the chin.

BASKET

Crochet it in thin string.

Begin with 6 chain stitch and join into circle with slip stitch (s.s. from now on).

FIG. 203

1st round: 1 treble into ring, 1 chain stitch. Repeat 5 times putting each treble into ring. Join into circle with s.s. into 1st treble.

2nd round: 1 treble into 1st treble of previous round, 2 chain. Repeat 6 times putting each treble into corresponding treble of previous round. Join with s.s. into 1st treble of round.

3rd round: 1 treble into 1st treble of previous round, 3 chain. Repeat 6 times putting each treble into corresponding treble of previous round. Join with s.s. into 1st treble of round.

4th round: As 2nd round finishing with s.s. into 1st treble of round.

Handle: Without breaking string continue and work 12 chain stitch. Join to 4th treble of last round with s.s. to form handle. Finish off end.

Mickey Monkey

A large toy. The one in the photograph is 16 in (*40·5 cm*) high. Requires time to gather the circles but there is less finishing off than in some of the others.

Shades of plain brown and patterns with brown predominating in brushed cotton, velveteen, linen and thin woollen cloth (if it is a firm weave) combine to form a variegated brown monkey. Head is plain brown cloth with yellow cloth face, hands and feet.

MATERIALS

Brown materials, plain or patterned	*Body.*	15 circles, diameter 6 in (*15 cm*).
	Arms and Legs.	100 circles, diameter 4 in (*10 cm*) (20 for each arm, 30 for each leg).
	Tail.	34 circles, diameter 2 in (*5 cm*).
	Emergency Doors.	3 circles, diameter 2 in (*5 cm*) 1 piece, 1½ in × 1 in (*4 cm × 2·5 cm*).
Brown cloth, plain	*Back of Head.*	2 pieces, each 5 in × 4 in (*12·5 × 10 cm*).
Yellow woollen cloth	*Face.*	2 pieces, each 4½ in × 3 in (*11·5 cm × 7·5 cm*).
	Hands.	2 pieces, each 3¾ in × 2¾ in (*9·5 cm × 7 cm*).
	Feet.	4 pieces, each 5 in × 2¾ in (*12·5 cm × 7 cm*).
	Ears.	4 pieces, each 2½ in × 1½ in (*6·5 cm × 4 cm*).
Firm cotton, any colour	*Reinforcement Circles.*	5 circles, diameter 2 in (*5 cm*). 1 circle, diameter 1 in (*2·5 cm*).
Firm cotton, brown or black	*Arm Junction.*	1 piece, 2½ in × 1½ in (*6·5 cm × 4 cm*).

Thread. Machine twist: Brown, yellow, black and orange.

12. MICKEY MONKEY

Filling.   Plastic foam chips.

Thin plastic foam sheeting or tweed:
Hands. 2 pieces, each 2 in × 1 in (*5 cm* × *2·5 cm*).
Feet.   2 pieces, each 4 in × 2 in (*10 cm* × *5 cm*).
Black Elastic. Body and Legs: 1 piece, 32 in (*81·5 cm*).
Arms: 1 piece, 19 in (*48·5 cm*). Both ¼ in (*6mm*) wide.
Tail: 1 piece, 13 in (*33 cm*) ³⁄₁₆ in (*5 mm*) wide.
If buying material. Brown cloth: 1⅝ yard (*1·7 metres*), 36-in (*90-cm*)
wide.

Yellow cloth: 5 in (*12·5 cm*) of 36-in (*90-cm*) wide.

CIRCLES   Gather circles for the body, arms, legs and 33 for the tail
(page 16).

REINFORCEMENT CIRCLES   Following page 18, attach the 1 in (*2·5
cm*) diameter circle to the smooth side of a tail circle. The 2 in (*5 cm*)
diameter circles: one to a body circle, four to leg and arm circles, all
to smooth side.

HEAD

Trace pattern. Cut two faces in yellow cloth and two heads in brown
cloth. Turn pattern over when cutting second pieces to make pairs.

Pin one yellow face to one brown head, matching points A and B,
wrong sides to outside. Backstitch together ¼ in (*6 mm*) from edge. Use
brown thread double. Open out to look as Figure 205. Repeat with
other two pieces.

Pin these two completed sections together, wrong sides to outside.
Backstitch together, using yellow thread down face seam and brown
thread on head. Leave X to X open at back of head. Turn back raw
edges round X X and tack down. Turn to right side.

Stuff with foam chips. Press stuffing to side of head to give breadth.
Ladder stitch, thread double, to close opening.

HANDS

Pattern and instructions as Clown's hands (page 85). Make in
yellow cloth, using yellow thread.

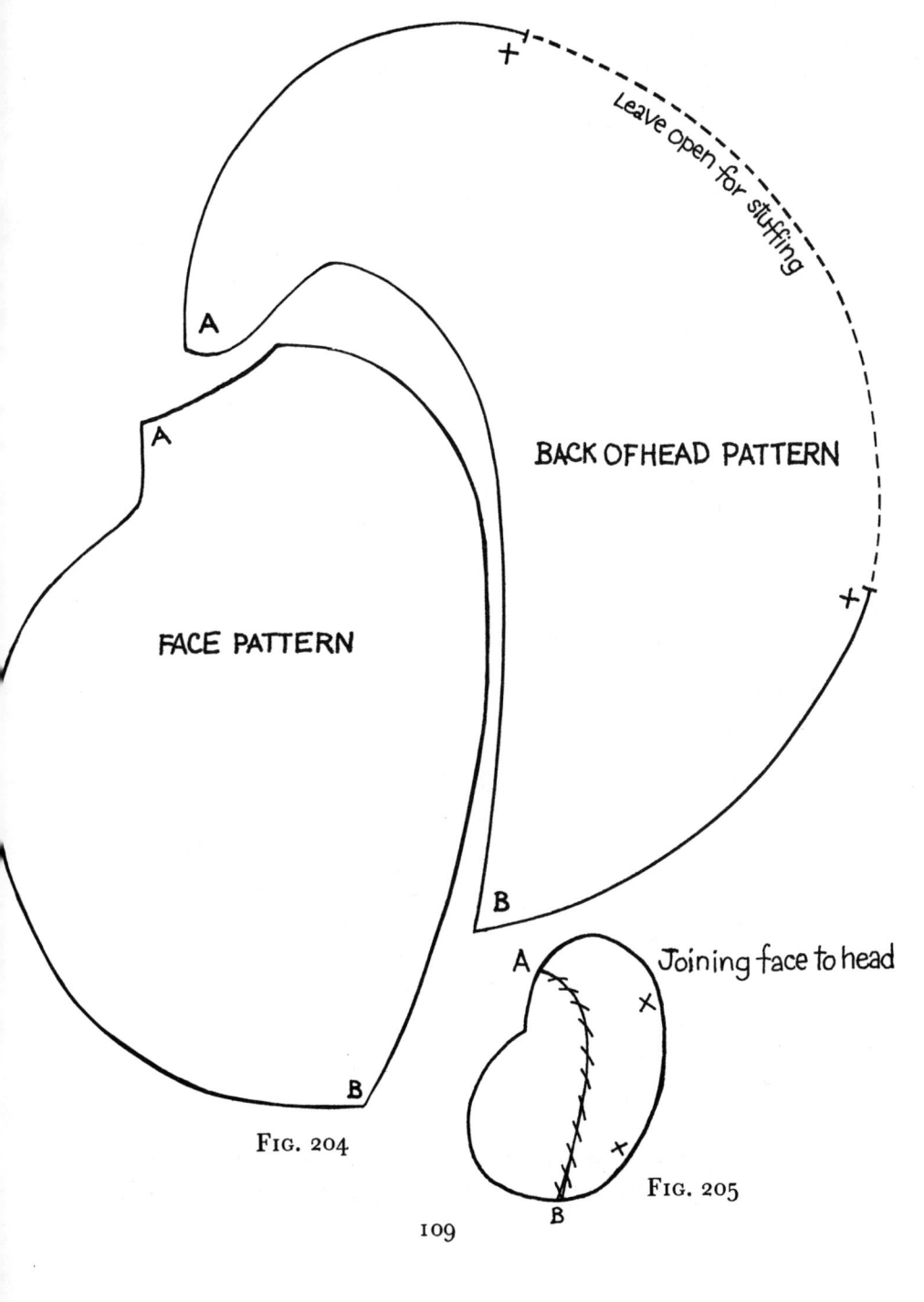

Leave open for stuffing

A

A

BACK OF HEAD PATTERN

FACE PATTERN

B

B

FIG. 204

A

Joining face to head

B

FIG. 205

Trace patterns. In yellow cloth cut four ears and four feet (feet cut to outer line). Turn pattern over when cutting second pieces, to make pairs.

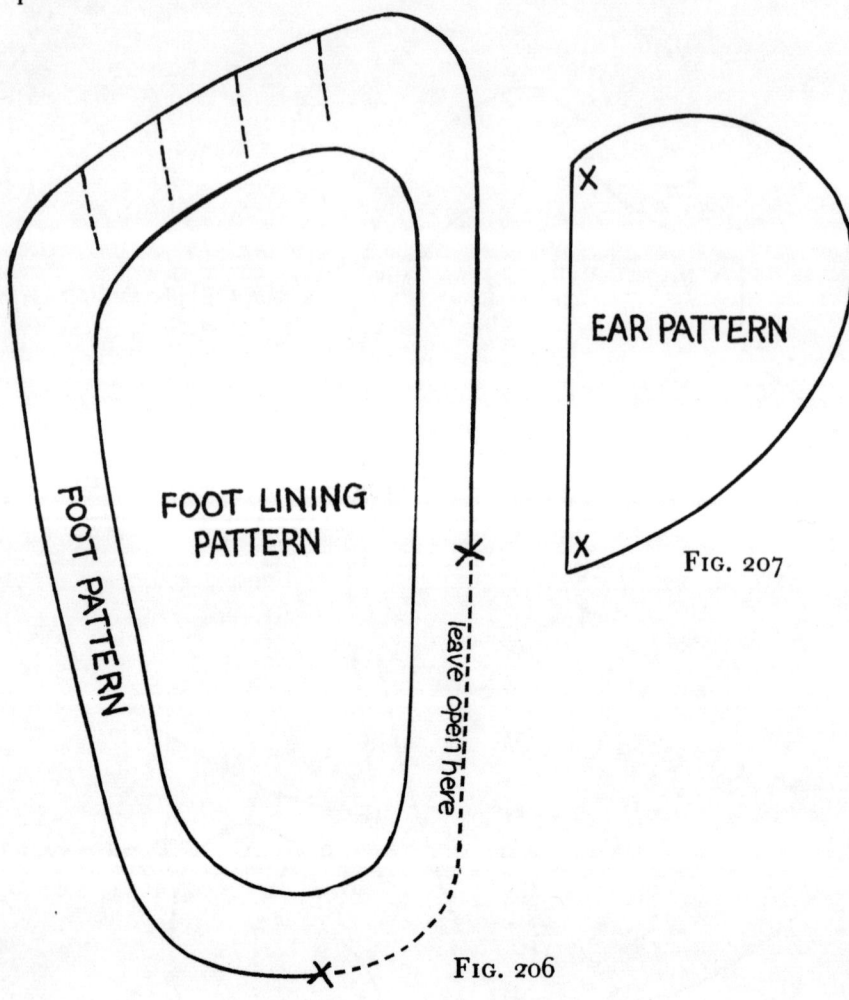

EAR PATTERN

FIG. 207

FOOT PATTERN

FOOT LINING PATTERN

leave open here

FIG. 206

Inner line is foot lining. Cut two pieces in foam sheeting or tweed. Place two yellow pieces together, wrong sides to outside. Use yellow thread double and backstitch $\frac{1}{4}$ in (*6 mm*) from the edge, leaving X to X open. Turn back raw edges round hole and tack down. Turn to right side. Slip lining inside foot. Ladder stitch to close opening, on ear and foot. Repeat with remaining pieces.

Toes: Using yellow thread double, backstitch four lines to mark toes (shown dotted on foot pattern). Work through all thicknesses.

TIP OF TAIL

Gather remaining tail circle. Pull up half tight. Slip in a little padding. Pull up tight and finish off thread.

ASSEMBLY
Tail

Fold 13-in (*33-cm*) tail elastic as shown (Fig. 208).

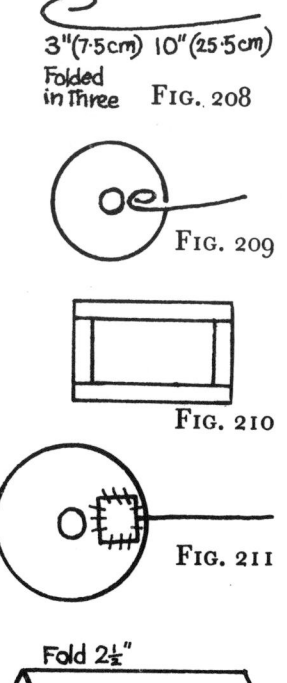

3"(7·5cm) 10"(25·5cm)
Folded in three   FIG. 208

Place folded end on smooth side of a body circle, near the centre hole. Main bit of elastic is on under side with folds above it.

FIG. 209

Using thread double, stitch very firmly through all thicknesses of elastic and both thicknesses of circle.

FIG. 210

Take the $1\frac{1}{2}$ in × 1 in (*4 cm × 2·5 cm*) piece of brown material. Turn over edges all round. Tack down.

Sew over the folded elastic to cover it and act as emergency door.

FIG. 211

Arms

Prepare arm elastic (page 22). Note that arm junction is longer than that shown on page 22. Sew to smooth side of a body circle.

Fold 2¼"

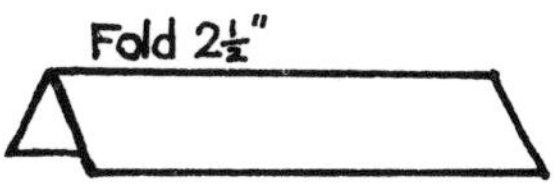

FIG. 212

For the rest of assembly follow basic method on page 23, in that order.

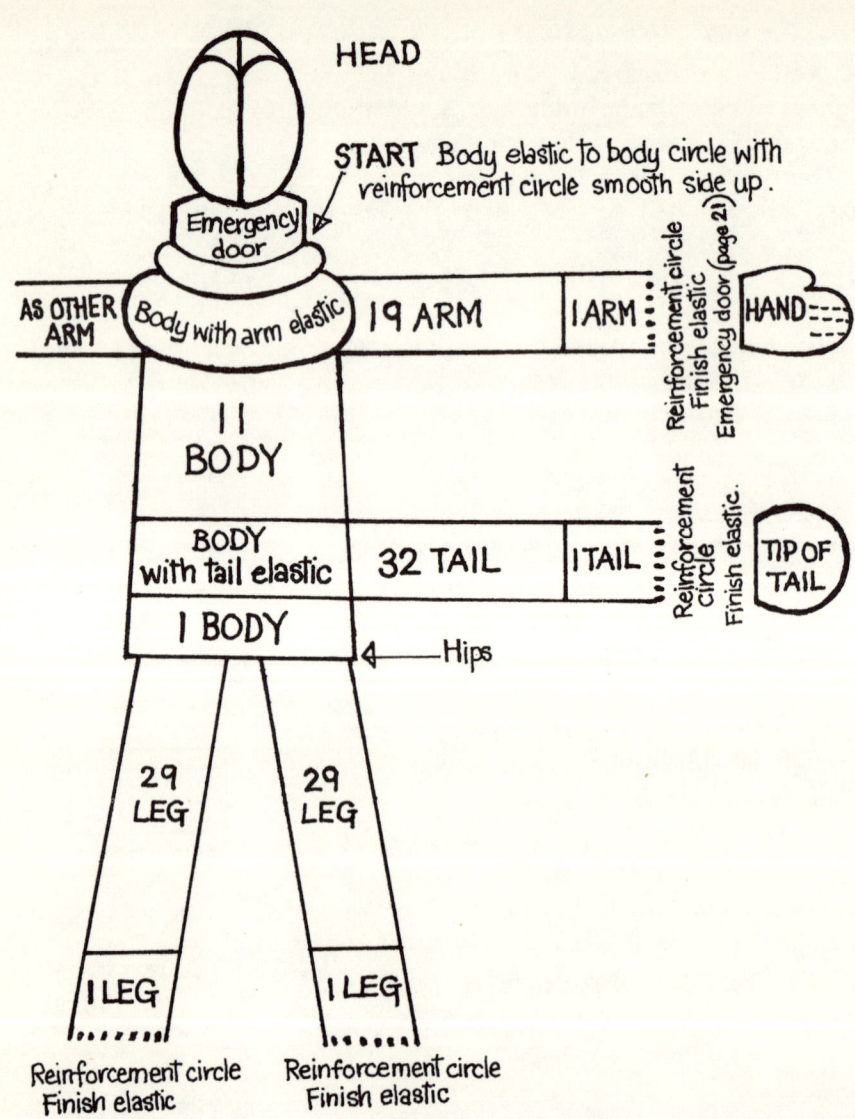

HEAD

START Body elastic to body circle with reinforcement circle smooth side up.

Emergency door

AS OTHER ARM | Body with arm elastic | 19 ARM | 1 ARM | Reinforcement circle Finish elastic Emergency door (page 21) | HAND

11 BODY

BODY with tail elastic | 32 TAIL | 1 TAIL | Reinforcement circle Finish elastic. | TIP OF TAIL

1 BODY

Hips

29 LEG   29 LEG

1 LEG   1 LEG

Reinforcement circle   Reinforcement circle
Finish elastic   Finish elastic

FIG. 213

All circles gathered side towards head, unless otherwise stated.

Hint. When sewing on head, take big shallow stitches the first time round to fix head in place as it is a little tricky to hold. Second time round take smaller stitches and dig right down through all thicknesses of top circle. For extra security, start a new thread for the second round: if one breaks the other will hold.

Assemble tail circles last.

Sew foot to each leg, as emergency door, big toes to inside to give him a right and left foot. Using thread double, ladder stitch twice round heel and across front of foot.

Sewing hand. Stitch through final circle the second time round as well as emergency door.

Ears

Use brown thread double to ladder stitch an ear to each side of head, on brown part. Sew twice round straight edge.

FIG. 214

FEATURES

Embroider as diagram, using black thread double.

Nose and Mouth. Do stem stitch to mark shape, then backstitch along three or four times to give prominent black line. Make large straight stitches from A to B.

Eyes. Black satin stitch, with a few orange stitches in centre.

FIG. 215

HIDING ARM JUNCTION If desired, use brown thread single to ladder stitch once along edge of two body circles to join them and conceal junction. Sewing need only go round half the circle.

Frisky Lamb

White acrilan fur fabric. Can use cuttings left over from other hand-
crafts. Or make it in white winceyette, when twice as many circles will
be needed as it is less bulky than fur fabric.

MATERIALS

White acrilan   *Body.*   6 circles, diameter 4 in (*10 cm*).
  fur fabric   *Legs and Tail.* 32 circles, diameter 2 in (*5 cm*) (7
  (washable)   for each leg, 4 for tail).

Head. 2 pieces, each 4½ in × 4 in (*11·5 cm × 10 cm*).

Ears. 4 pieces, each 2½ in (*6·5 cm*) square.

Leg Junctions. 2 pieces, each 1 in (*2·5 cm*) square.

Firm cotton,   *Reinforcement Circles.* 1 circle, diameter 2 in (*5 cm*).

any colour   5 circles, diameter 1 in (*2·5 cm*).

Thread. Machine twist: White and black.

Linen or button thread: White.

Filling. Plastic foam chips or, when cutting out the circles keep the fur clippings, cut them into small bits and use them.

Elastic. Body: 1 piece, 11 in (*28 cm*). Legs: 2 pieces, each 14 in (*35·5 cm*). All $\frac{3}{16}$ in (*5 mm*) wide.

If buying material. ¼ yard (*23 cm*) of 54-in (*1·4 metres*) wide material; but ⅓ yard (*30 cm*) of 54-in (*1·4 metres*) wide will make two lambs.

CIRCLES   Gather circles for body, legs and tail (page 16).

REINFORCEMENT CIRCLES   Following page 18, attach the 2 in (*5 cm*) diameter circle to the gathered side of a body circle. Attach the 1 in (*2·5 cm*) diameter circles to the smooth side of five leg and tail circles.

HEAD AND EARS

Trace patterns. With pile stroking in direction of arrow cut two pieces for head, turning pattern over when cutting second piece to make a pair. Cut four pieces for ears.

Place two pieces together, wrong sides to outside. Using thread double, backstitch ¼ in (*6 mm*) from edge. Leave dotted edge A to B open.

Ears. Turn back and tack down raw edge. Use small stitches and they need not be removed. Turn to right side. Slipstitch to close opening.

Head. Turn back raw edge and, using thread double, gather round the hole, leaving end of thread hanging. Turn to right side. Stuff with foam chips or fur clippings. Pull up gathering thread and finish off.

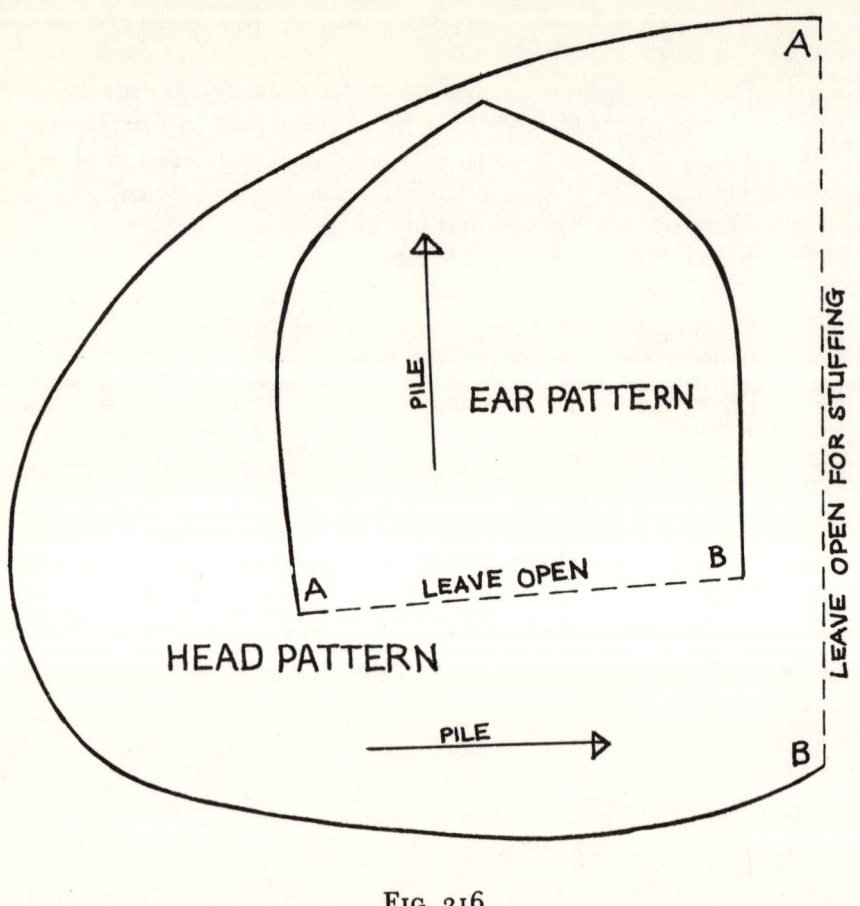

FIG. 216

ASSEMBLY

Prepare the two leg elastics (page 22). As the leg junctions are cut in fur fabric do not turn over the raw edges. Slipstitch edges with thread used single. Sew one prepared elastic to the smooth side of a body circle for back legs. Leave other elastic aside for front legs.

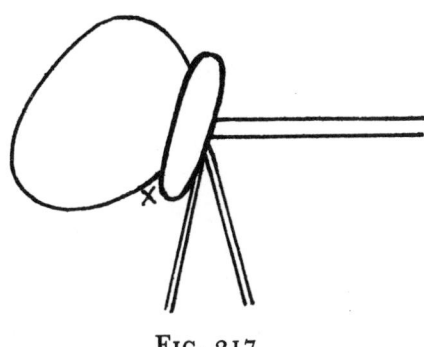

1. Attach body elastic to body circle which has reinforcement circle on gathered side (page 19).

2. Sew prepared elastic for front legs to smooth side of this circle below body elastic. Position junction so that body elastic lies either horizontally or vertically to the ground.

FIG. 217

3. Sew on head to act as emergency door. Place head so that lower edge is just above edge of body circle (X on diagram). Ladder stitch round twice, using linen thread double. Take stitches well into fabric, not just through fluff.

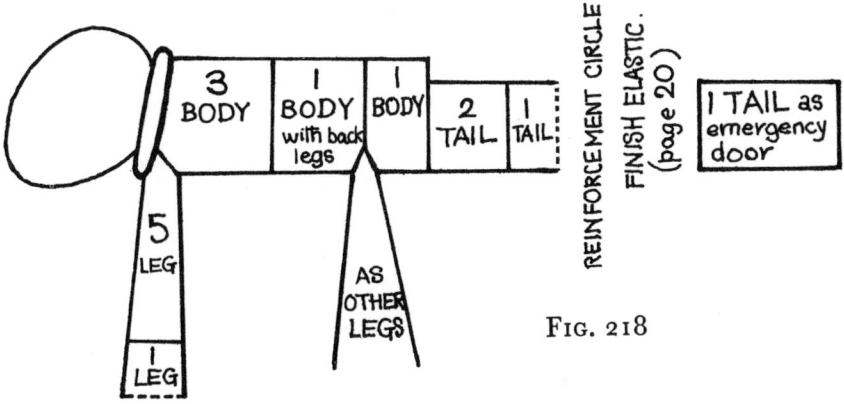

FIG. 218

REINFORCEMENT CIRCLE

FINISH ELASTIC

(Page 20)

4. Assemble rest of circles as Figure 218 above, all gathered side towards head. Finish tail before threading legs.

Ears

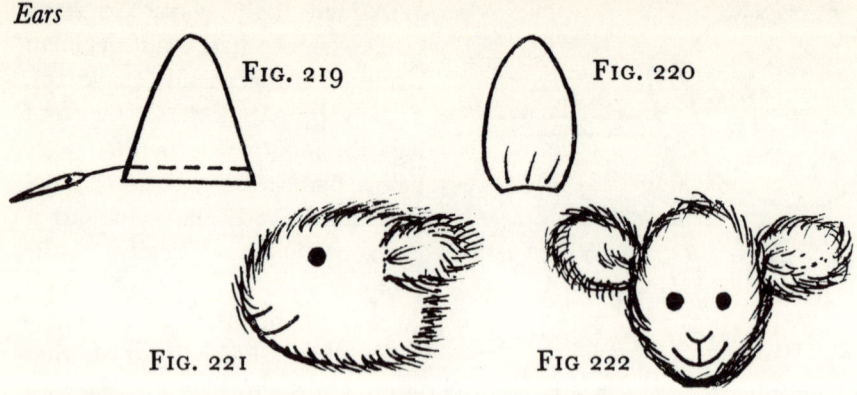

FIG. 219

FIG. 220

FIG. 221

FIG 222

1. Using thread double, gather along front of ear (Fig. 219).
2. Pull up gathers. Fasten off.
3. Using thread double, ladder stitch one ear to each side of head. Ear sticks straight out sideways. Stitch round twice, stitching well down into base fabric.

FEATURES

Using black thread double, satin stitch eye on each side of head. Stem stitch curved line for mouth. Two straight stitches form V for nose. Go over them more than once.

Singh the Tiger

Mixed oranges and yellows with black for stripes. Orange head. Stripes can be arranged to suit material available. Duster cloth gives ideal soft feel and colours. Black cotton is effective for stripes.

MATERIALS

	Oranges and yellows	Black cotton	Firm cotton, any colour
Body. Circles, diameter diameter 6 in (*15 cm*)	14	6	—
Legs. Circles, diameter 2½ in (*6·5 cm*)	40 (10 each leg)	16 (4 each leg)	—
Tail. Circles, diameter 2 in (*5 cm*)	9	5	—
Feet. Circles, diameter 2 in (*5 cm*)	8	—	—
Head. Circles, diameter 4 in (*10 cm*)	2	—	—
Ears. Pieces, 2¼ in × 1¾ in (*6 cm × 4·5 cm*)	4	—	—
Reinforcement Circles. Diameter			
2 in (*5 cm*)	—	1	1
1 in (*2·5 cm*)	—	—	6
Leg Junctions. Pieces 1½ in (*4 cm*) square	—	2	—

Thread. Machine twist: Orange, yellow and black.
White for whiskers.
Stranded cotton: Black.
Filling. Plastic foam chips.
Thin plastic foam sheeting or tweed:

14. SINGH THE TIGER

4 circles, diameter 1½ in (*4 cm*).

Elastic. Body: 13 in (*33 cm*). Legs: 2 pieces, 15 in (*38 cm*) each. All ¼ in (*6 mm*) wide.

Tail: 8 in (*20·5 cm*) ⅟₁₆ in (*5 mm*) wide.

If buying material. Orange: 2 pieces, 24 in (*60 cm*) square or ⅚ yard (*76 cm*) of 36-in (*90-cm*) wide material.

Black: ⅓ yard (*30 cm*) of 36-in (*90-cm*) wide material.

CIRCLES Gather circles for body, legs and tail (page 16).

REINFORCEMENT CIRCLES Following page 18, attach the black 2 in (*5 cm*) diameter circles to two orange body circles, one to a smooth side and the other to a gathered side; four of the 1 in (*2·5 cm*) diameter circles to the smooth sides of four orange leg circles; one of the 1 in (*2·5 cm*) diameter circles to the gathered side of an orange tail circle and one to the smooth side of a black tail circle.

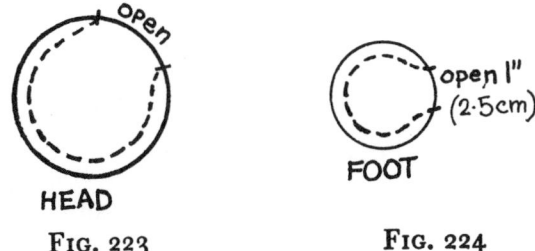

FIG. 223   FIG. 224

Place two circles together, wrong side to outside. Backstitch ¼ in (*6 mm*) from edge.

Head. Leave good sized opening for stuffing.

Foot. Leave about 1 in (*2·5 cm*) of opening.

Both. Turn down raw edges round opening and tack. Turn to right side.

Head. Stuff with foam chips. Do not overstuff: it should be a flattish head. Do not worry if head does not look a perfect circle. Foam is difficult to shape exactly. Ears and features will disguise any deficiency in shape.

Foot. Slip in 1½ in (*4 cm*) diameter circle of foam sheeting or tweed.

Both. Ladder stitch to close opening.

ASSEMBLY

Prepare the two leg elastics (page 22). Sew each one to the smooth side of a black body circle.

Start. Stitch body elastic to orange body circle that has reinforcement circle on gathered side (page 19).

Head goes slightly above circle (see Fig. 225). Put foot of reinforcement circle to base of head, just behind seam. Head covers reinforcement circle. Position it so that body elastic lies either horizontally or vertically to the ground. Ladder stitch round twice with thread double.

Thread on circles as shown, all with gathered side towards head. Thread body first, then tail; join body and tail (see Fig. 225); then thread legs.

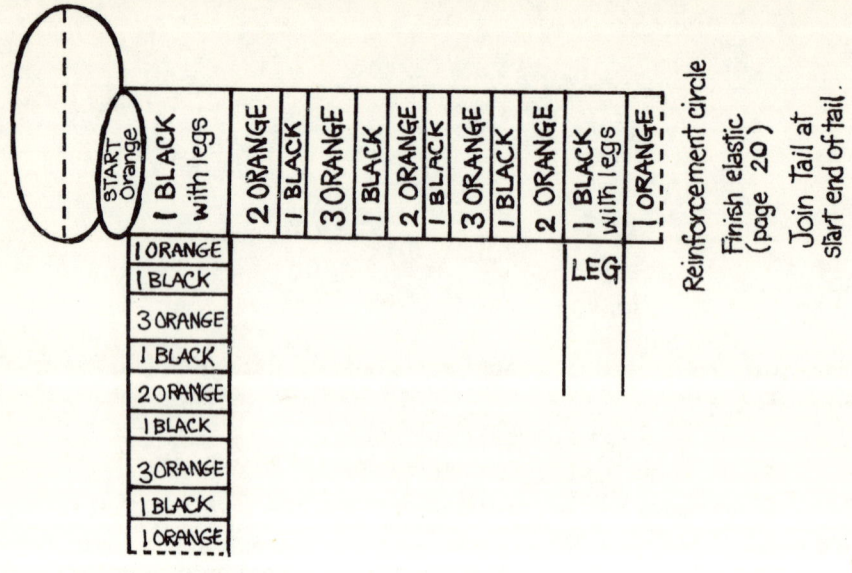

START Orange

| | 1 BLACK with legs | 2 ORANGE | 1 BLACK | 3 ORANGE | 1 BLACK | 2 ORANGE | 1 BLACK | 3 ORANGE | 1 BLACK | 2 ORANGE | 1 BLACK with legs | 1 ORANGE |

1 ORANGE
1 BLACK
3 ORANGE
1 BLACK
2 ORANGE
1 BLACK
3 ORANGE
1 BLACK
1 ORANGE

LEG

Reinforcement circle
Finish elastic (page 20)
Join Tail at start end of tail.

Reinforcement circle
Finish Elastic
(page 20)

TAIL

START elastic (page 19)

Reinforcement circle.

| 1 ORANGE | 1 BLACK | 3 ORANGE | 1 BLACK | 2 ORANGE | 1 BLACK | 3 ORANGE | 1 BLACK |

Reinforcement circle
Finish elastic (Page 20)

1 BLACK as emergency door

Fig. 225

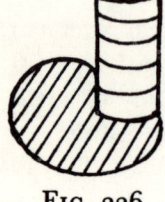

Fig. 226

Join body and tail. Ladder stitch round twice with orange thread used double. All elastic should be covered, but border of black reinforcement circle on body will show, making another black stripe.

Sew foot to each leg, as emergency door, back of leg to back of foot. Use orange thread double. Ladder stitch round twice.

122

Toes. Use black stranded cotton (three strands). Long lines show division of toes so put them on front and back of foot (one big stitch taken round). Short lines are claws so sew them on front only.

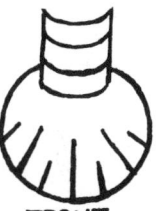

FIG. 227   FRONT

EARS

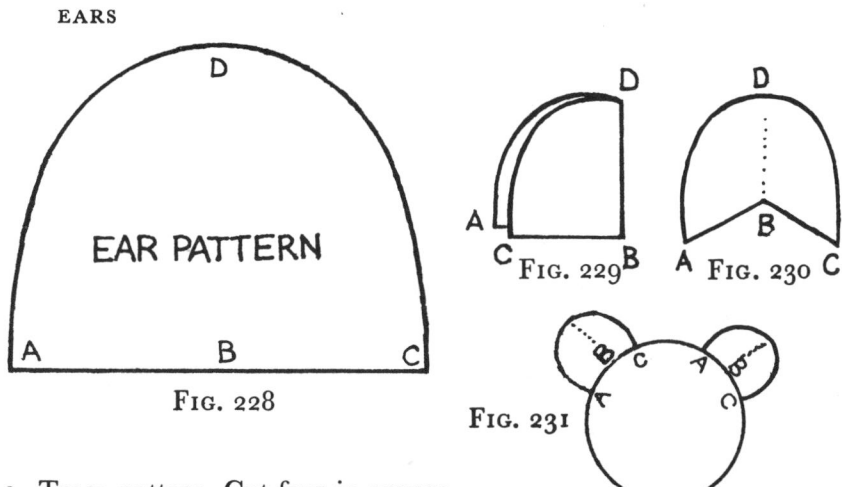

EAR PATTERN

FIG. 228

FIG. 229

FIG. 230

FIG. 231

1. Trace pattern. Cut four in orange.
Place two together, wrong sides outside. Using single thread, backstitch CDA. Turn over raw edges round ABC. **Tack down. Turn to right side. Slipstitch to close ABC.**

2. Fold ear in half. Using thread double, take about three stitches at B to hold the two sides together (Fig 229).

3. This gives the ear a curve when opened out.

4. Place ears on seam line of head, one each side. Ladder stitch round ABC twice, using thread double.

FEATURES

Sew with black stranded cotton (three strands). Satin stitch eyes. Stem stitch elsewhere. Use single strand to mark sides of nose, shown dotted. Use orange thread double to put dot in centre of eye. Do not worry about position of markings, the diagram is only a general guide.

Fig. 232

WHISKERS

Use white thread double. Take a long length. Make two tiny stitches at X to fix thread, then leave a big loop as shown. Take another two tiny stitches at X to fix the loop. Make another loop and another two stitches at X.

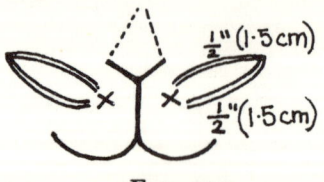

Fig. 233

Carry thread through to X on other side of nose and repeat. End with two tiny stitches, then finish thread.

Cut ends of loops. There will be eight single threads sticking out at each side and the tiny stitches should prevent them from pulling out.

Joseph in His Coat
of Many Colours

Joseph is made of knitted squares, instead of gathered circles of material. Double knitting' wool is used, or thinner wool used double.

His coat is a mixture of bright colours. Trousers are dark blue, but different shades of dark blue will mix together. Head and hands are pink winceyette; feet are black cotton.

MATERIALS

Bright coloured wools	*Coat, body.*	20 squares, approximately $2\frac{1}{2}$ in (*6·5 cm*) square.
	Coat, arms.	48 squares, approximately $1\frac{1}{2}$ in (*4 cm*) square (24 for each arm).
	Arm junction.	8 stitches, 6 rows stocking stitch, in one of the body colours.
Dark blue wool	*Trousers.*	48 squares, approximately $1\frac{1}{2}$ in (*4 cm*) square (24 for each leg).
Wool	*Hair.*	Small ball black.
	Mouth.	Red 4-ply, 9 in (*23 cm*).
	Eyes.	Royal blue.
Pink winceyette	*Head.*	2 pieces, each $5\frac{1}{4}$ in × $4\frac{1}{4}$ in (*13·5 cm × 11 cm*).
		2 pieces, each $5\frac{1}{4}$ in × $2\frac{1}{2}$ in. (*13·5 cm × 6·5 cm*).
	Hands.	2 pieces, each $3\frac{3}{4}$ in × $2\frac{3}{4}$ in (*9·5 cm × 7 cm*).
	Ears.	4 pieces, each $2\frac{1}{4}$ in × $1\frac{1}{4}$ in (*6 cm × 3 cm*).
Black cotton	*Feet.*	4 pieces, each $4\frac{1}{2}$ in × 2 in (*11·5 cm × 5 cm*).

15. JOSEPH IN HIS COAT OF MANY COLOURS

Firm cotton,   *Reinforcement Circles.* 5 circles, diameter $1\frac{1}{2}$ in (*4*
   any colour   *cm*).

Knitting needles. No. 9.

Thread. Machine twist: Pink, red and black.

Filling. Plastic foam chips.

    Thin plastic foam sheeting or tweed:

    Hands. 2 pieces, each 2 in × 1 in (*5 cm × 2·5 cm*).

    Tweed: *Feet.* 4 pieces, each 4 in × $1\frac{1}{4}$ in (*10 cm × 3 cm*).

Elastic. Black is better than white as it will be less conspicuous in the
    dark trousers.

    Body and legs: 1 piece, 28 in (*71 cm*). Arms: 1 piece, 19 in
    (*48·5 cm*). Both $\frac{1}{4}$ in (*6 mm*) wide.

If buying material. Pink winceyette: 6 in (*15 cm*) of 36-in (*90-cm*) wide
    material.

KNITTED SQUARES

Body squares. Cast on 12 stitches. Knit 20 rows garter stitch. Cast off.

Arm and trouser squares. Cast on 8 stitches. Knit 14 rows garter stitch.
Cast off.

Arm Junction. Described in MATERIALS.

REINFORCEMENT CIRCLES

Prepare as on page 18. Sew one to a body square, choosing the colour
of square you wish to put next to head. Sew two to dark blue squares for
ends of trousers. Sew two to arm squares. For each arm choose a colour
that has another square knitted in the same wool for use as emergency
door. Left and right arms need not be alike.

HEAD

1. Trace pattern.

   Front of head. Cut two pieces as shown with nose. If material has right
and wrong side turn pattern over when cutting second piece.

   Back of head. Fold back nose at dotted line to leave pattern, as shown

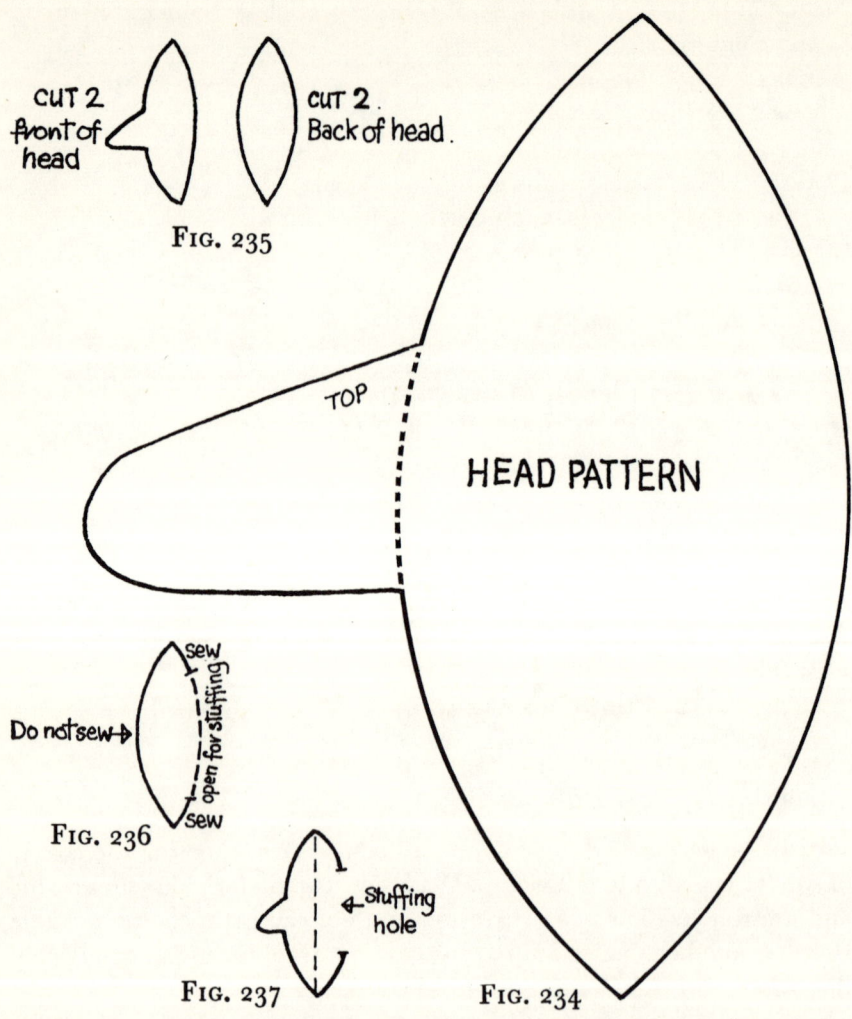

CUT 2
front of
head

CUT 2.
Back of head.

FIG. 235

TOP

HEAD PATTERN

sew
open for stuffing
Do not sew →
sew

FIG. 236

Stuffing
hole

FIG. 237

FIG. 234

in Figure 235. Cut two pieces.

2. Place two fronts, with noses, together, wrong sides to outside. Back-stitch along nose side ¼ in (*6 mm*) from edge, using thread double.

3. Repeat with the two pieces for back of head, but leave an opening for stuffing (Fig. 236).

4. Turn back raw edges round stuffing hole. Tack down.

5. Lay these two sections together. Backstitch right round edge (shown dotted on Fig. 237).

6. Turn to right side. Stuff with plastic foam chips. Do the nose first with tiny chips put in a little at a time and pushed down with a blunt-ended knitting needle. Ladder stitch along hole to close it, using thread double.

HANDS AND FEET

Pattern and instructions as for Clown (pages 85–7). Hands made in pink winceyette with fingers stitched in pink. Feet made in black cotton, stitched with red round the edge.

ASSEMBLY

Threading elastic through wool. Knitting is open enough to allow elastic through without making a special hole.

Arm Junction. Fold it round centre of arm elastic with smooth side of knitting next to elastic. Stitch edges.

Using thread double, stitch it firmly to the body square that is made from the same wool. Put it just below centre point to allow for body elastic.

Arm Emergency Door. Ladder stitch hand to centre of arm square that is to be emergency door. Using thread double, sew round twice.

Follow basic method of assembly on page 23, with squares threaded as Fig. 238. Sew elastic at START so that cast-on or cast-off edge of square will come to front.

Sew foot to each leg to act as emergency door. Using black thread double, ladder stitch twice round heel and across front of foot.

Arm Emergency Door. Use wool to sew square to its neighbour to cover reinforcement circle and finish of elastic. Oversew outer edges. Take a stitch through the elastic to hold it to the centre of the square.

Wrist. Take a few stitches through centre of the two squares that are sewn together to hold them close together. (Not too many stitches or you will defeat the emergency door idea.)

Arm Junction. Sew the square with arm junction to the one below it.

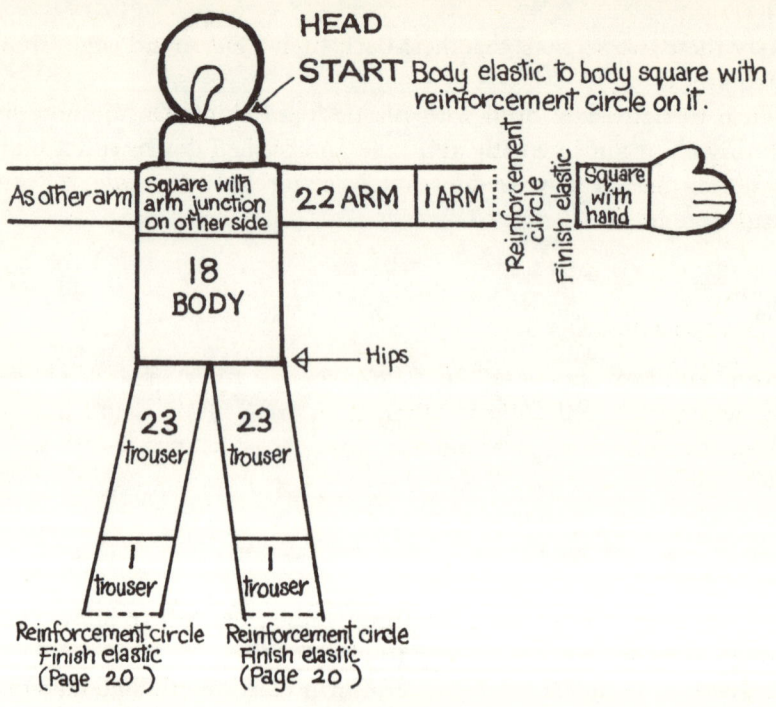

FIG. 238

Oversew, thread or wool, round outer edges. When sewing along sides take a stitch through the elastic to keep it to the centre of the side.

EARS

Trace pattern. Cut four in pink winceyette. Make as Wee Willie Winkie's ear (page 54). Ladder stitch one to each side of head, on side seam, about halfway down head. Sew along front, back, then front again.

HAIR

Make as Wee Willie Winkie (page 56).

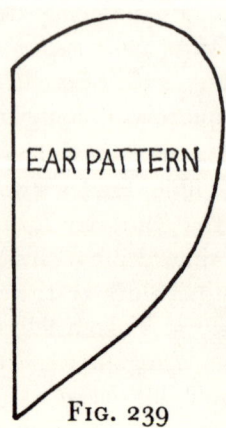

EAR PATTERN

FIG. 239

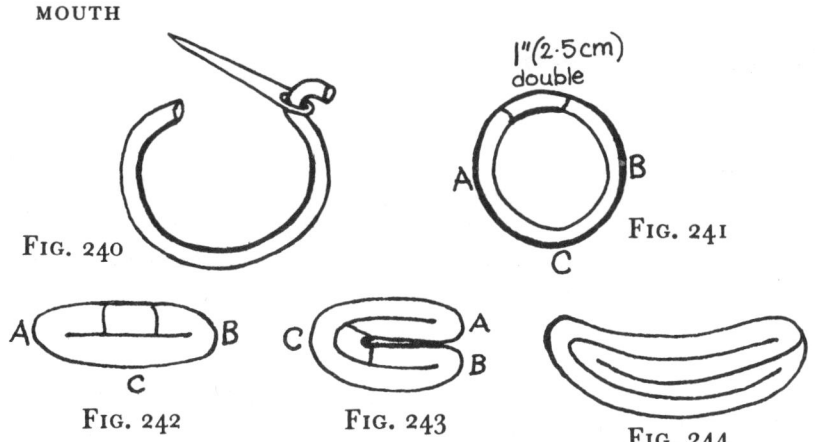

FIG. 240   FIG. 241

FIG. 242   FIG. 243   FIG. 244

1. Put darning needle on to one end of the 9-in (*23-cm*) length of red wool.

2. Thread through other end of wool for about 1 in (*2·5 cm*). Pull out needle. Wool will now be in a continuous length (Fig. 241).

3. Fold in half (Fig. 242).

4. Fold in half again (Fig. 243). This gives four strands lying side by side.

5. Lay this piece on face, ends curving up slightly at ends to give a smile (Fig. 244). Using red thread single, take small stitches here and there through the wool and face until the mouth is completely caught down. Stitches should be practically invisible as they sink into the wool.

EYES

FIG. 245   FIG. 246   FIG. 247

Satin stitch centre first with black wool.

With royal blue wool make straight stitches round centre.

Eyebrows: With black wool sew three or four stem stitches. Work along twice.

Hint. Start and finish black wool among hair.

Knitted Toys

All the floppy toys can be made in knitting.

Knit small squares in garter stitch and just thread them on elastic. The result is square instead of round, but the cuddly feel and mobility of the toy are the same.

Joseph, in his Coat of Many Colours, is given as an example of a knitted toy.

To make any toy in the book in knitting, gather one fabric circle and then knit squares to that measurement.

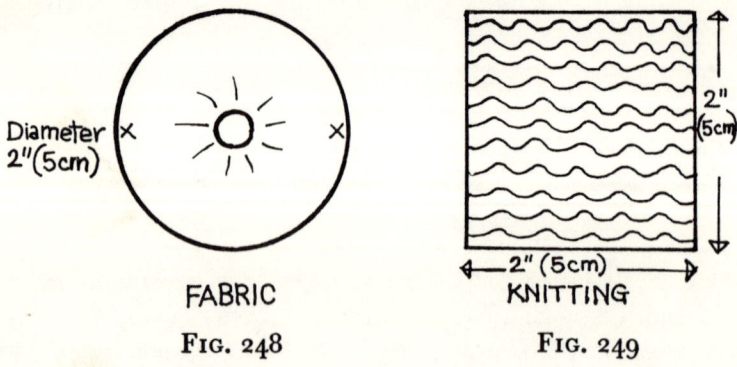

FABRIC

Fig. 248

KNITTING

Fig. 249

By a similar calculation Joseph can be converted to gathered circles of fabric.

Stitches

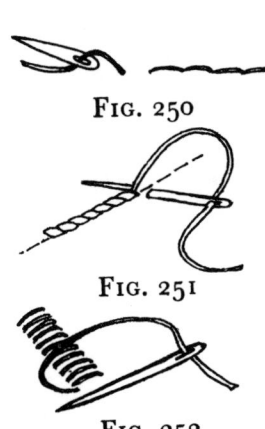

FIG. 250

Backstitch

FIG. 251

Stem Stitch as in Crewel embroidery.

FIG. 252

Satin Stitch Straight stitches worked closely together.

FIG. 253

Oversewing

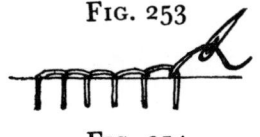

FIG. 254

Blanket Stitch. Put needle through fabric, then up under thread at edge of fabric.

FIG. 255

Gathering
1. Take small, straight stitches.

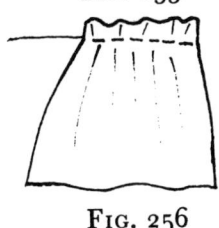

FIG. 256

2. Pull thread tight so that material gathers up in folds.

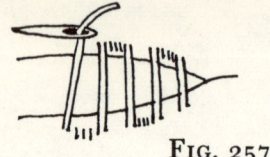

FIG. 257

Ladder Stitch

Makes it easy to join awkward parts.

Take one small straight stitch on one part, then a small straight stitch on the other part. Keep the stitching moving in the same direction. Pull the thread tight every three or four stitches and the stitches will lace up and disappear, leaving a neat join that is very strong because there is no thread on the surface to be worn away. The Figure shows the stitches before the thread which laces it together is pulled tight.

Imagination with Material

Variegated Toys
Choose a basic colour. Different shades of that colour, and patterns which have that colour predominating, blend together to give an over-all effect in the basic colour Examples: Sneaky Snake (greens) and Mickey Monkey (browns).

Multi-coloured Toys
No basic colour is needed. Any colours or patterns can be combined and no two circles need be alike, yet a gay harlequin effect is achieved. Example: Tumbler the Clown.

Threaded-to-order Toys
Chosen colours can be threaded to achieve a particular effect. Example: Footballer, with blue and white circles alternately to make a striped jersey, then all blue circles for pants, pink for knees and blue and white again for striped socks.

FIG. 258

FIG. 259

MIX AND ADAPT

Play around on these themes.

Make a dozen green variegated snakes and each one will look different according to the fabrics used and order of threading. Try variegated orange snakes, red snakes, black and white snakes. Try multi-coloured snakes, using odd circles of any colour. Try threaded-to-order snakes making them striped—perhaps threading three brown, one yellow along the length.

A toy like Santa Claus which must be red, can be variegated red and still look like Santa. No red? Make him in green and call him a Gnome.

These are a few examples. Most of the toys can be adapted in these ways to use whatever materials you have available.